IS YOUR LOVE LIFE SO-SO . . . OR NO-NO?

Turn off the TV and learn how to be a star in your own love story. Discover how the secrets revealed in this book can change your life—even as they have transformed the lives of the women who received these letters from their men:

"How can I put into words how I've felt being with you the last few weeks? I feel like a teenager again. I can't wait to come home. . . . The change in the way you treat me makes me want to spoil you for the first time in years. Thank you for bringing back the woman I married."

"You are the most fantastic woman alive. I've never felt this close to anyone before. . . . Sometimes I wonder if there are any other men who are lucky as I am. Now that I've found you, I cannot imagine living without you."

"After all these years, I'm falling in love with you all over again. . . . I only hope I can begin to give you what you've given me in the past few weeks. Because of you I feel alive for the first time in many years."

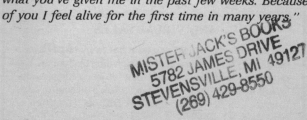

Light His Fire

HOW TO KEEP YOUR MAN PASSIONATELY AND HOPELESSLY IN LOVE WITH YOU

Ellen Kreidman

A DELL BOOK

Published by
Dell Publishing
a division of
Bantam Doubleday Dell Publishing Group, Inc.
666 Fifth Avenue
New York, New York 10103

The trademark Dell ® is registered in the U.S. Patent and
Trademark Office.

ISBN: 0-440-20753-3

Reprinted by arrangement with Villard Books

Printed in the United States of America

Published simultaneously in Canada

February 1991

10 9 8 7 6

RAD

DEDICATION

This book is dedicated to my husband, Steve, who is the kindest, most loving, patient, and supportive man I know. I am the luckiest woman in the world to have the honor and choice of being his wife. He is everything a woman could ever dream of, or hope to have, in a husband. He is my inspiration, my rock, my whole world. Without him, this book would never have been written.

WARNING!!!

Do not read this book unless:

- You are a woman who wants to captivate and mesmerize a man for the rest of his life.
- You are a woman whose marriage is beginning to crumble and you want to turn it completely around.
- You are a woman about to be married who wants to continue having those *butterflies* in your stomach and a love affair for life with your mate.
- You are a woman whose failed marriage has prevented you from entering a new relationship because you're fearful of more pain and loss.
- You are a woman who is nervous about a relationship because you have never been in one and lack the knowledge to make it work.

I REPEAT—DO NOT, UNDER ANY CIRCUMSTANCES, read the following material unless you want complete control over the destiny of your love life!

FOREWORD

Most women today do not know how to keep a man interested and committed to a long-term relationship. After reading this book, you will have the ability and the power of keeping a man passionately and hopelessly in love with you. You will be all the woman he will ever need or want in his lifetime.

Some of you have a tough enough time trying to balance your professional life with your personal life without reading a book that is long and heavy on theory. Knowledge, research, and explanations are important, but if you don't know how to apply them in your own life, what good are they?

What you need is a step-by-step guide on exactly what to do and say to have a love affair with the man of your choice for the rest of your life. This is exactly why I wrote this book. *Light His Fire* has examples you can relate to, is quick and easy to read, provides easy-to-understand principles, and tells you exactly what to do and say for immediate results.

At the beginning of Chapter 2 through 7, you will read some of the personal letters my graduates have shared with me, letters they received from their husbands or boyfriends as a result of Light His Fire seminars.

I have not tampered with punctuation, grammar, spelling, or sentence structure in any of them, because I want you to read the actual note or letter the way it was written. Obviously, I have changed their names to protect their privacy.

I have included these notes and letters to prepare you for the results that the principles I teach will have, and to show you that the average woman is completely capable of changing her attitude and behavior and then benefiting from the results.

The men who have written these letters are not writers, poets, or English majors. They are just ordinary men who were so moved by their mates' new behavior that they were inspired to reveal their feelings. I know you will enjoy them as much as I did.

It is my hope that you will receive your own love letter from the man in your life. Now, let's get started together on your new romantic adventure.

ACKNOWLEDGMENTS

I will be forever grateful to all those people in my life who have contributed to turning my hopes and dreams into reality.

In particular, I am grateful to my mother—who gave me the love and nurturing a child needs in order to feel wanted, valuable, and special; and to my father —who worked so hard all his life to provide me with an education and an environment where I could reach, stretch, and grow.

I am grateful to my children—not a day passes that I don't feel blessed and privileged to be their mother. Jason, my strong-willed, opinionated, honest, caring, and energetic son; Tiffany, my intuitive, gentle, kind, creative, and original daughter; and Tara, my compassionate, sensitive, idealistic, devoted, and generous daughter—all have helped me to write this book in ways both big and small.

I am grateful to Frances Wright, whose daily encouragement, friendship, and belief in me over the years has not only helped to validate my dreams, but has helped to fill my seminars with students.

I am grateful to Sandra Caton, whose endless hours of dedication, energy, and creative talents helped shape my manuscript into a work worthy of consideration by my publisher; and to Judy Semler, my literary agent, who made its publication feasible. Judy's constant optimism, encouragement, and professionalism turned all the possibilities into probabilities.

I am grateful to Diane Reverand, my editor, whose brilliant and intuitive mind helped sharpen and enhance my manuscript. Her knowledge and insight kept me focused on the theme of the book and helped me to achieve my ultimate goal.

And last, but not least, I am grateful to all of the graduates of Light His Fire. This book could not possibly have been written without their enthusiasm and their belief that what I had to say was important and worthy of their valuable time. I thank them all from the bottom of my heart for their letters and testimonials of the personal successes they achieved as a result of my program.

CONTENTS

1
KNOWLEDGE GAINED
FROM EXPERIENCE

*I*f I wanted to know how to earn a great deal of money, I wouldn't ask someone who was struggling to make ends meet for his opinion. I'd ask someone who was wealthy.

If I wanted advice on child-rearing, I wouldn't ask someone who had no children or whose children were delinquents. I'd want to talk to someone who had raised happy, loving, successful children to find out what they did.

I'd much rather listen to Nobel Prize winner Linus Pauling, who is in his nineties and speaks from personal experience, tell me how to keep my body healthy, than a twenty-five-year-old whose knowledge is strictly out of a textbook.

Talk is cheap. Everybody's willing to give advice,

whether they know what they're talking about or not. The human jaw is the most used "muscle" in the entire human body! But sound advice from a knowledgeable source is not so easy to come by.

If you wanted to stop smoking, would you sign up at a clinic where the person in charge lit one cigarette after another as he tried to convince you that it was a piece of cake to quit smoking? Of course not! Nobody's that gullible.

It's time our society began to question our criteria for what constitutes an expert in any field. I'd much rather listen to Jane Fonda, Raquel Welch, or Debbie Reynolds (who are all in great shape) tell me what to do with my body, than a muscle-bound "expert" with a degree in physical education. Richard Simmons talks with experience and compassion on how to lose weight and diet properly because he's done it. His personal experience makes him a more effective teacher than the nutritionist with a Ph.D. who received all his knowledge from a textbook. As far as I'm concerned, it's time to recognize a new group of experts with the initials K.G.F.E. after their names, signifying *K*nowledge *G*ained *F*rom *E*xperience.

If you want advice on how to have a happy relationship, one that is filled with romance, respect, devotion and love, you have to ask a happily married couple who are already living that life. With this premise, I created Light His Fire, a relationship workshop based on the real-life experiences of people with K.G.F.E. degrees. They are the true experts in the field of love and life.

HOW IT ALL BEGAN

The first years of my marriage were nearly perfect. My husband and I had two beautiful children and were very well off financially. So well off that I had live-in help and we traveled frequently all over the world. We were happily anticipating our third child when the bottom fell out of my idyllic life. My husband lost his job! Months went by with no job offers and none in sight, and our financial picture began to change. Finally, we faced bankruptcy, and if that wasn't enough to cope with, my husband's father died and my mother-in-law asked to come live with us.

I spent most of my pregnancy crying and feeling very sorry for myself. By the time my son was born, we had depleted our entire savings and had relocated to a very small house. Eventually, my husband found another job, one that paid considerably less than what he had been making before, and my mother-in-law moved into a nearby apartment, but I remained angry and filled with self-pity.

Extremely depressed, I was on my way home from the supermarket one afternoon when I had an experience that was to change my view of life forever. As I gripped the steering wheel and sat waiting for a traffic light to change, I began sobbing and desperately asking over and over, "Is this all there is to life? Is this it?"

Suddenly, I became aware of a voice inside me saying, "Yes, Ellen. This is all there is. For things to change *you* have to change."

I was shocked that I had actually gotten an answer

to my question! It was as if there were another presence within me.

Although I didn't understand it at the time, I had tapped into an inner source, a guide within me that would direct me wherever I needed to go if I would let it. Since that day, I have confirmed that we are *all* our own best therapists and our own best medical guides, if we can just learn to listen to our instinct and do what we know we need to do. *We have all the answers within us.*

All of a sudden it became very clear to me that my life and my happiness were my responsibility. My fulfillment was going to have to come from inside me, not from some outside source. As a phrase I've heard since then says, "If it's to be, it's because of me."

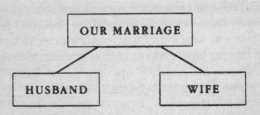

It was at that stoplight that I decided to stop feeling sorry for myself and to make some necessary changes. Once I came to grips with the fact that I was responsible for my life, I realized that my marriage was in jeopardy. Both my husband and I had been so busy feeling sorry for ourselves that we had failed even to consider the other person, much less put forth any effort toward communication or intimacy.

It was clear that if my marriage was to survive, I had to put some thought, time, and effort into it.

In spite of all the other pressures on me, I chose to concentrate on my marriage, because I had invested too many years just to give up without a fight. I began to see my marriage as a separate entity. There was my husband, myself, and the marriage. The marriage required more effort than I had been giving it. I thought back to the time before we were married, remembering that there were many times when we were dating that one or the other of us was unhappy. We had family pressures, school pressures, social pressures, and money pressures, and yet our relationship worked.

It worked because our relationship was separate from ourselves. A relationship, like a corporation, consists of a combination of personalities but has a life of its own. Just as a corporation requires dedication and concentration if it is to grow, so too does a relationship between two people. Perhaps I didn't feel like a walk on the beach, but the marriage *required* a walk on the beach. I certainly didn't feel like a weekend alone with my husband, but the marriage *required* a weekend alone together. A call just to say I was thinking about him and loved him was very hard to make, but the marriage *required* that call. A candlelight dinner was very difficult to plan, but the marriage *required* that kind of atmosphere. Making love was the furthest thing from our minds, but the touching and healing that comes from that union was *required* by the marriage.

Everything we do in life requires work, why shouldn't marriage? We take continuing education classes to improve our professional lives and to qualify for salary increases and promotions; why not do the same for our personal lives?

As I looked for ways to improve my marriage, I began to wonder why some couples stay together and others call it quits. Later that year, I began to research this subject seriously. During the course of my research, I interviewed hundreds of couples who had been married a minimum of ten years and as many as fifty-five years. What I found was that it's not what happens to us that determines the quality of our lives with someone else. It's what we do about what happens that will determine the quality of our lives together. I found that most relationships experience similar problems. They all have their share of boredom, routine, financial problems, problems with the children, problems with the relatives, and major life disappointments. The difference was that problems which might cause other relationships to fall apart brought these couples closer together.

NEW OUTLOOK, NEW OPTIONS

Armed with a new outlook and new information, I began to apply what I had learned to my own life and to share it with other women. Unsure if what I had to say would make a difference in anyone else's life, I rented a small office on a month-to-month basis, furnished it classroom style, and in May 1981, I held the first formal class of Light His Fire.

Since then we have moved into much larger quarters, and I have lectured to thousands of women on how to put fun, growth, excitement, and communication into their relationships. Today, Light His Fire is a six-week workshop in which women learn that they can't light someone else's fire unless they feel good about themselves and come from a position of strength and knowledge, not weakness, subservience, or ignorance. Four years ago, as a complement to the women's classes, I started teaching men how to Light Her Fire.

I also lecture to groups and organizations. Many forward-thinking companies—companies that realize the importance of balancing one's career with a fulfilling personal life—have asked me to speak to their employees. Just as the medical profession has begun to accept the mind-body connection and the need to treat the whole person—physically, emotionally, and mentally—corporate America is beginning to see the importance of addressing the personal issues in its employees' lives as well as the professional issues. Understanding that our personal life does affect our professional life, companies, which until recently have only dealt with their employees' professional lives, have begun to fill the void by presenting programs such as mine. They are beginning to understand that there is certainly more reason to earn an exceptional income if there is an exceptional person in your life.

I have written this book for all those women who found it geographically impossible to attend my six-week program, and for all those women who took my program but wanted a book to keep as a refresher or to give to their sisters, friends, mothers, and other women to whom my class was inaccessible. Now, at last, I can say yes when my students ask me if I have a book. Now, all those who are unable to attend my lectures can learn the principles that I've found to prevail in all the wonderful relationships I've researched. If you will apply these principles to your own relationship, the results will be astounding. My goal is to show you how you can have the relationship you've always dreamed about—one filled with love, mutual respect, communication, romance, excitement, and passionate sex. It's all up to you. *You have that power!*

As for my credentials, I have degrees in psychology and education, but that really doesn't matter. More important is that I have been married twenty-three years to the same man and I have three happy, well-adjusted children. Most important of all is that I practice what I teach and *I still light my husband's fire!*

FRANKIE'S STORY

Both of Frankie's parents were alcoholics and were divorced by the time she was two years old. After their divorce, Frankie and her two brothers spent the next ten years living with their mother in shacks and cars just trying to survive. As Frankie's mother's drinking became worse, she could no longer cope with the responsibility of raising the children, and Frankie's father was forced to take over. However, he also was unable to handle raising teenage children, and one day he dropped Frankie off at a police station and asked them to keep her there to teach her a lesson. Frankie told the authorities about the abuse she and her brothers had endured for years. After hearing her story, they decided to send the children to live in Juvenile Hall.

At Juvenile Hall, Frankie pleaded with anyone who would listen to find her a decent home. Finally, after three months, she was placed in what would become the first of the many foster homes in which she lived until she turned eighteen. Frankie says what got her through all the tough, lonely, miserable days and nights was the dream that someday she would be married to a wonderful man, and have children and a home of her own.

That dream became a reality when she met her "knight in shining armor," but after she and Norm were married, she quickly realized how unprepared she was for marriage. Her lack of role models, experience, and knowledge led to frustrations that eventually caused her physical illness. For years, she searched everywhere looking for answers, but friends, psychologists, TV, and books never seemed to provide her with the tools she needed. She finally learned to settle for a mediocre marriage. "After all," she reasoned, "I have two beautiful children, and a husband who comes home with a paycheck and provides a roof over our heads." And yet, Frankie always felt something was missing.

Frankie had been married for eighteen years when a friend insisted that she go to one of my lectures. Her initial reaction was, "I don't need this. He does! I've read all the books, taken all the classes, and even been in therapy." Reluctantly, Frankie signed up for my six-week class.

The changes were immediate and profound. Light

His Fire not only revolutionized Frankie's marriage, it also improved her relationship with her children, and most important, it changed the way she felt about herself. For the first time in her life, Frankie was not getting theory but concrete examples of what she needed to do to improve her relationship as well as her life. She learned how to get rid of her anger so that she could achieve romance, communication, fun, and intimacy in her life. As the weeks went by, Frankie began to see immediate results. She learned more about her husband in those six weeks than she had in the previous eighteen years. She began to have a love affair with her husband, and the butterflies she had felt at eighteen returned at age thirty-six. Once Frankie had the proper tools to improve her relationship, her fear, frustration, and loneliness disappeared.

This book is for every woman who has ever dreamed of happy endings and believed that fairy tales can come true. I believe that if you will apply the knowledge in the pages that follow, you'll feel the same fulfillment and strength that Frankie now has, the strength that comes from being a woman in love and creating your own destiny.

For all those women who come from a dysfunctional home, there finally is a way to function in your own home. Frankie used to think she was the luckiest girl in the world to have Norm as her husband, but now she can honestly say that Norm is the luckiest man on earth to have her as his wife.

HAPPY ENDINGS

Frankie's story is not unique. Hundreds of women have told me how they have benefited from Light His Fire.

- Mary began to receive love letters addressed to her after the first few classes. She received two offers of marriage and three dozen roses all in the same month.
- Jane had always been afraid of men. With her new understanding and insight, she was actually able to realize a lifelong dream to go into business as an image consultant to businessmen.
- After she'd done just three homework assignments, Cindy's lover of four years proposed marriage.
- At the beginning of the workshop, Julie, a powerful, dynamic woman, was in a relationship that was going nowhere. By the time Julie graduated, she had learned how to channel her power and energy into a good relationship, and she had a new man in her life who didn't require her to settle for less.
- When Sharon first came to class, she was convinced that there was nothing I could teach her about relationships that she didn't already know. Six weeks later, she had love messages and roses all over the house. Obviously, she hadn't known some of the things she needed to know.
- Bonnie's marriage was over and the divorce was almost final. She only came to class to keep her daughter company. After six weeks, Bonnie and

her husband were on a second honeymoon—a world cruise!

These are some of the success stories of ordinary women who now live extraordinary lives. They are women from all walks of life—married, single, professional, homemakers, old and young. If it can happen to them, it can happen to you.

YOUR PROMISE, MY PROMISE

I want you to promise me that, from this moment on, you will take full responsibility for your own happiness. You can always find someone else who is willing to tell you what you should or shouldn't do, but no matter who it is—your husband, a parent, a friend, or even a neighbor—you're always better off making your own decisions regarding your happiness. If you focus on improving yourself, you'll automatically build a better relationship with your mate. If, on the other hand, you focus on improving your mate, it will lead to disappointment and failure. We can never improve someone else's behavior—only our own.

In any love relationship, there is a chain reaction. If you do some changing, your mate will react to the change in you. For example, Anna, a student in one of my classes, told me that every Friday night her husband went out with "the boys," and would always come home drunk around three in the morning. Sometimes he even approached her for sex (not lovemaking) in this condition. Anna dreaded Friday nights, and by Wednesday she would typically start nagging her husband to stay home the coming Friday and the fight would start. On one particular Friday evening, as Anna's husband got ready to leave, she gave him a big hug and kiss and said, "Honey, I've been very selfish. You work hard all week and you really do deserve a night out. I want you to have fun tonight, and when you get home, I'll be waiting up and have a snack ready for you."

Her husband looked at her and shouted, "Don't wait up, and don't have a snack waiting! I don't know what time I'll be home!"

With that, he slammed the front door and left. That night, for the first time in sixteen years, he came home before midnight and had only had two beers. Although he automatically reacted to his wife in the same way that he always had, he must have said to himself after he left, "Gee, that was really nice of her to say, and look how I reacted. I feel really awful (and probably a little guilty)." I don't care if it *was* guilt that made him change his usual pattern; what's important is the result—he came home early and was not drunk.

My promise to you is that as you apply the principles taught in this book, you will see incredible, almost magical, changes take place in your life and, most important, in your mate. He will be more loving and romantic. Your communication with him will improve. You will be showered with gifts and other tokens of his appreciation for you. You'll feel special and important. Most of all, you will experience more inner peace and happiness than you have ever known before.

In addition, you will discover that my Light His Fire

principles and techniques have a ripple effect—the same principles behind developing a more loving relationship with your husband, when applied to your children, will make them more considerate and helpful. When applied in the workplace, your boss will become more appreciative and admiring. When your personal love life works, everyone else benefits from your happiness.

Thousands of women who have taken my class have learned that:

- You don't have to settle for a mediocre life.
- You don't have to settle for a run-of-the-mill relationship.
- You don't have to settle for weeds when you can have a garden.
- You don't have to settle for crumbs when you can have a feast.

Before these changes can occur, there must be new attitudes and behaviors on your part. In the chapters that follow, you will be given the information you need in order for this to happen. You will be asked to say and do things that may be a little uncomfortable, or perhaps even foreign to some of you, but I know that once you try them, the rewards will be fantastic and the results will be astounding.

Moonlight walks on the beach, romantic candlelight dinners, hugs, kisses, secret glances, and gifts are all waiting for you. Your new responses to his old behaviors will make you the heroine in the romantic novel of life.

2

DO I QUALIFY?

*L*ois was one of those women who had decided to call it quits after twenty-two years of marriage. "Enough is enough," she said when I first met her. "I want to light *him* on fire—not light *his* fire," she said.

Lois couldn't understand why her husband didn't realize that her way of thinking and doing things was the right way. Once she understood that their differences were not a matter of right or wrong, and gave her husband permission to be himself, she experienced a tremendous change in their relationship. In response to her new accepting attitude, her husband took her in his arms and said, "Now, this is the woman I married." A short time later, her husband sent her flowers for the first time in twenty-two years, with the following note:

How can I put into words how I've felt being with you the last few weeks? I feel like a teenager again. I can't wait to come home to the new woman in my life. The change in the way you treat me makes me want to spoil you for the first time in years. Thank you for bringing back the woman I married.

All my love,
Stan

The first principle in making a love relationship work is to love someone for who he is, not what you fantasize he should or could be. This is love in its purest form—the kind of love most women give to their newborn babies. There are no qualifications necessary to receive this love; it's automatic.

Only as the baby begins to grow do we start to use the word *if*: "I'll love you *if* you get good grades." "I'll love you *if* you make me proud." "I'll love you *if* you do what I say."

We do the same thing with our mate. In the very beginning, when you first fall in love, you truly do love that person for who he is. Later your love becomes conditional: "I'll love you if you earn more money." "I'll love you if you will be more outgoing." "I'll love you if you will stop watching sports on TV so much." "I'll love you if you'll just be a better parent."

If, as a lover or parent, you are offering love that is conditional—love that always has an *if* attached to it—then it becomes necessary for your mate or child to qualify for your love. Conditional love requires a person to wonder whether he is worthy, deserving,

meets the requirements, or is otherwise eligible for
your love. We have to qualify for a job, *not* a relationship! Unqualified love means there are no prerequi-
sites, no contingencies, no requirements for your
love. It is a gift given with no strings attached. *What
you see is what you love!* This is not the case in your
professional life. There you have to meet requirements, pass inspection, make the grade; but it cannot
be the same with your personal life. Qualified love is
too impersonal.

YOU'RE ALWAYS BEING TESTED

Do you realize how often, and in how many different
ways, you are tested by your mate? When a man asks
his wife, "What happens if I get this promotion and
we have to move to another state?" most wives respond with, "What do you mean, move to another
state? We aren't going anywhere! I've lived next to
Joan for ten years and I'm not about to move!" What
he wants to hear is, "I don't care where we live. We
could live in a tent or on a desert island, and I'd be
happy as long as we're together." A response like this
allows room for communication. Now, he can tell you
about his mixed feelings and the torment he may be
going through. If a man feels truly loved, then he'll
want to make the best decision possible for all concerned, and he'll also want to be the best person he
can be for you.

Another serious problem men ask about is "What
happens if I don't get that raise?" Too often wives
respond with, "Why would you ask that question?"

"Don't be so negative," "If you continue to work hard, you'll get the raise!" "How are we supposed to keep the kids in college and keep up with inflation if you don't get a raise?" or "If you don't get the promotion, you'll just march into your boss's office and tell him you deserve it!"

What your man really needs to hear is "Nothing will happen. We'll manage. We'll just tighten our belts and we'll get by. All that matters is that we are together and I love you."

That was my response when my husband lost his job. As we eventually faced total financial ruin, there was not a day that went by that my husband didn't ask, "What's going to happen if I can't get another job? What are we going to do?"

Until I realized that my marriage was in jeopardy, I bought into my husband's fear and worried right along with him. When I stopped feeling sorry for myself and was able to focus on my husband's needs, my response to his worry changed. I reassured him that as long as we were together, nothing else mattered. "We started with nothing, and we can do it again. We'll get through this together," I told him. With just a little support on my part, he was able to respond lovingly to me and to find the inner strength necessary to fight our circumstances. Many years later, when my husband was reflecting back on those trying times, he took me in his arms and told me how much my love and consistent support had meant to him. "It took so much pressure off me," he confided.

The principle of loving a man for who he is was learned by a student named Kathy at precisely the right time for her to put it into practice. The night we discussed this in class, Kathy returned home to find her husband standing in front of the mirror, running his fingers through his hair. "I'm starting to lose my hair," he told her. "See, my hairline is already receding. What's going to happen if I become bald?" he fretted.

Kathy put her arms around him and said, "Nothing is going to happen. I love you and I'm very glad you're mine. You're the handsomest man I know— with or without hair. Besides, bald is sexy. Look at all the women that lusted after Yul Brynner."

Without the lesson on unconditional love, and the knowledge that her husband's question was a test, Kathy would have responded much differently, perhaps saying something like, "Well, you could always get a transplant. It's very common, and it's not really terribly expensive these days."

Worse yet, she might even have giggled and said, "I can't picture you bald. That would be awful!"

Instead, she was able to reassure her husband of her love, and he responded by kissing her and telling her how much he loved her.

Penny, a student in her fifties, talked shyly about her husband's fear of impotence. She said that as she and her husband were about to make love one evening, John pulled away and said, "I can't." Penny's first impulse was to respond with anger.

That's great, she thought. At the end of the month, we're going on a cruise, and he can't make love. He means he doesn't want to!

Instead, with a great deal of compassion, she said, "That's okay. What's important to me is to just feel your arms around me, holding me."

John said, "I'm fifty-eight years old. What if I can't ever make love again?"

(There's the test again.)

Penny answered, "Nothing is going to happen. I love you now, and I'll always love you, no matter what. You've been under so much pressure lately that it's no wonder you can't relax."

When her husband wondered aloud if he should go to a doctor, Penny reassured him.

"No," she said. "I think you just have to learn how to relax."

She stroked his hair as she reaffirmed her love, telling him, "The only thing that matters is how much I love you. I just want you to hold me," and they fell asleep in each other's arms.

A few weeks later, I received a letter from Penny telling me she was thrilled with the results of her unconditional love. They had a wonderful time on their ten-day cruise, even making love every night like a couple of newlyweds.

I remember another woman in my class who raised her hand and told us that she went to counseling to verbalize her feelings. She felt her husband loved her only when the house was spotless, but what she really needed was to know he loved her in order to have the strength to keep the house clean. You might have to read that a few times before you understand what feeling loved really means.

Anyone who feels he is loved for what he does or what he has, feels *used*, not loved. Love should be given as a gift, with nothing asked in return. It should say, "I love you because you're you, and I'm so lucky to have you in my life!"

Since my husband had been a competitive swimmer in high school, my children all started swimming when they were very young. When my son was about twelve years old, he couldn't stand the sport anymore and wanted to quit. He came to me one evening saying how much he wanted to quit, but he was afraid if he did, his dad and I would hate him.

I put my arms around him and said, "We could *never* hate you. We love you because you're our son." Then I asked him if he would still love his dad if he lost his job and wasn't earning any money.

He gave me a puzzled look and said, "Yes, of course I'd still love him."

Then I asked if he'd still love me if I stopped cooking. (Little does he know that it's a real possibility!)

Again he said, "Yes, of course."

Then I asked if he'd love his sisters if they stopped swimming.

He answered yes again.

"So what we have or don't have, do or don't do, has nothing to do with your love for us, does it?" I asked.

"No," he replied.

"Well, it's the same with us. We'll always love you, no matter what you do or don't do, have or don't have. You've been swimming because you're really good at it, your heart and lungs are in great shape, and your father really loves the sport. But understand this—whether you swim or not has nothing to do with our love for you."

Eventually, he began to play soccer, a sport he still enjoys. How lucky I was to be able to reinforce my unqualified love to my child and to give him choices.

When those little boys grow up to become our

mates, they still need reassurance that no matter what they do or don't do, have or don't have, are or are not, they will still be loved. They need to know that our love will not disappear.

TRASH OR TREASURE?

You're probably wondering how you can possibly love someone unconditionally when there are so many things about him that you don't even like. The answer is to do some attitude adjustment. You must fine-tune your thinking. You have to understand that to be human is to have faults as well as virtues; that no one is going to be perfect or a carbon copy of you.

What you define as a fault is very subjective—one woman's trash is another woman's treasure. Something you consider to be a fault in your husband may actually be seen by another woman as a virtue. For example, if you're upset because your mate is too ambitious, there are many women who consider their mates to be too complacent and who would give anything if they were more aggressive. For every woman who feels that her husband spends too much time with the children, there are just as many who feel they don't spend enough and care only about themselves. There are women who complain that their husbands are sex maniacs who want to make love all the time. Other women would give their eyeteeth to have such a man, because their husbands aren't interested in sex. For every trait you consider negative, there is another woman out there who would look at it in a positive way.

They don't say that "love is blind" without good cause. When you first fell in love, you just saw his positive attributes. Only later did you start to see all of his negative traits. In the beginning, you might have seen him as gentle and easygoing—later you tell him he's apathetic and dull. In the beginning, you loved the fact that he was so affectionate. Years later, you think of him as oversexed. You were attracted to him because he was a sophisticated traveler. Now, he's a compulsive nomad. He may go from sports fan to sports maniac. You loved his confidence, now he's conceited.

The interesting thing is that, if he were to become involved with a new woman, she would see only his positive qualities. He might start to feel good about himself again for the first time in many years when he's with her.

WHY MEN FALL IN LOVE

The majority of men I have interviewed, whether married or single, agreed that they felt captivated by that special woman who was able to make them feel stronger, more capable, more intelligent, sexier, or more knowledgeable than they had felt about themselves before these women came into their lives.

For example, Michael, who was quiet and withdrawn, told me he had always been a loner. In a group situation, he always listened intently but never felt confident about giving his opinion. When he met Melinda, he recalls the feelings he had about himself after a few dates.

"She always commented that she loved my easygoing nature," he said. "Melinda was very high strung and she told me she always felt calmer and more peaceful when she was with me. For the first time in my life, I started feeling good about my personality."

A man named Patrick related how different he felt with his ex-wife and his present girlfriend.

"I have a very high sex drive, I guess. With my ex-wife, I always felt like I was a sex maniac. She'd complain about how abnormal I was and continually tell me to take a cold shower, go for a walk, or go to the gym to work off my urges."

"My girlfriend, Donna, on the other hand, makes me feel wanted. She tells me how affectionate and passionate I am, and how she loves that about me."

He ended by saying, "Being with a woman who was incompatible had me beginning to doubt myself. It's so good to feel like I'm normal."

Hank, a stockbroker who considers himself an expert in the field, remembers that every time he'd go out on a date, he'd try to impress the woman he was with with his knowledge. "I'd even give them free financial advice," he said.

"It wasn't until Marilyn came into my life that I felt like a genius," he continued. "She was amazed at how much I knew about different companies. She'd listen for hours as I explained the transactions of the day. Marilyn made me feel so intelligent because she appreciated who I was."

Sam is a traveling salesman. "I'm on the road at least four days a week, and my old girlfriend complained, whined, and argued about how much I was gone. I married my wife, Suzie, because she felt that my job was so exciting and I was such an interesting man, traveling to all those places. Suzie was, and still is, eager for me to return home and tell her, in detail, about my experiences that week. She makes me feel like I'm the most adventurous man alive.''

Ken stated that he never felt he was particularly good-looking until Karen came into his life. "I've never been a 'ladies' man,' and had almost no dates in high school," he said. "Karen and I have been married twenty-seven years, and I still feel like I'm the best-looking man alive when I'm with her. Karen always tells me how handsome I am and what a great body I have.

"Who am I to argue with someone as wonderful as my wife, who still sees me as her 'Adonis'?" he asked, as he blushed and rolled his eyes.

Patrick is a bodybuilder who met his wife at the gym where he used to work out. "I can still remember the day we met. Ann was working out on a machine, next to me. She turned to me and said, 'How do you make that look so easy? I'm struggling, and you make it look like it's a piece of cake.' "

"How could I not get to know this woman?" he continued. "After six years of marriage, she still gloats at my muscles. Every time we see a muscular guy on the beach, Ann turns to me and whispers, 'You're in better shape than he is.' I guess when it comes right down to it, I feel sexy when I'm with her. She even told our three-year-old daughter how lucky she is to have a daddy in such great shape," Patrick concluded proudly.

Are you beginning to get the picture? **Men fall in love because of the way they feel about themselves** when they are **with you**. One of the reasons my husband fell in love with me was because I always laughed at his jokes. He felt great around me because I thought he was so funny. (By the way, I still laugh at his jokes.) Usually, when a man no longer feels good about himself when he is with you, he finds another woman. That's what an affair is all about. It's not that he's in love with the other woman—it's that *he's in love with the way he feels about himself* when he's with the other woman. So, if you want to recapture your love affair with your husband or mate, you have to make him feel good about himself. Otherwise, the best you can hope for is to trade him for a new man who has different strengths and different weaknesses.

Suppose you did leave your present man for a new "knight in shining armor." This new man is everything your previous man was not. For example, he's sensitive and caring, but because he is, he has many friends who call constantly to ask for advice or help. Or perhaps he has a twelve-year-old daughter with whom he spends too much time, or he has an ill mother who demands too much of his energy and money. You may have fallen in love with him because he is verbal and your last man was not. But because he is verbal, he always monopolizes the conversation and you can hardly get a word in, and he is unaware of your feelings because he is so wrapped up in himself. Or, finally you meet a man who earns a wonderful living, but because he's successful, he's gone a great deal of the time. So now you feel lonely, though you didn't before when you were with a man who came home every evening at six. Maybe you've found the most romantic man alive—a true Casanova. The problem is that he loves all women and his flirting arouses tremendous jealousy in you. I know one thing for sure—the longer you know any of these men, the more annoying traits you will see—unless you learn to change your attitude instead of your man.

YOUR HERO FOREVER

For every action there is a reaction. For every trait there is a response to that trait. You must learn to react in a positive way and stop being judgmental. When you concentrate on a man's strengths instead of his weaknesses, you get more positive behavior.

During an appearance on the Johnny Carson show, Mort Sahl once said, "Women always marry a man and hope he'll change. Men always marry a woman and hope she'll never change."

Women seem to go into a relationship saying, "I know there are a lot of things about him that I don't like, but wait until I get through with him. You won't even recognize him."

Men, on the other hand, say, "When I'm with this woman, I feel like a king. It's wonderful. I hope she never changes. I always want to feel like this." That, by the way, is why he wants to marry this woman. He wants to feel like her hero for the rest of his life.

Once you begin to focus on all the things you con- sider weaknesses and try to change him, the love you had in the beginning starts to die.

NO PAIN, NO GAIN

Wouldn't it be simple if we fell in love with someone who was exactly like us—same interests, same personality, same sensitivities? Absolutely not! Do you know why? Because we're all on this journey called life in order to learn and grow, and you learn nothing when you're always in complete agreement with another person. Conflict leads to growth—it does not have to lead to divorce.

Many years ago, I heard Bruno Bettelheim lecture on the family, and someone asked him what he felt the American family's biggest problem was. He answered that the biggest problem with the American family is that they think there *should be no problems.* I agree completely. Most men and women feel that conflict or problems mean the relationship cannot work. I believe, on the contrary, that a relationship cannot work unless there *are* problems and conflict.

We have friends from India whose marriage was arranged. They are happier than any other couple I know, because they went into marriage knowing it's an ongoing process. Marriage is not an end, it's a beginning.

In fact, our Indian friends don't even think of themselves as human beings, because that implies stagnation. Rather, they think of themselves as *human becomings,* which implies growth. So, all of you *human becomings* out there who are interested in growth must understand that there will always be conflict, especially because we are almost always attracted to someone who is different from ourselves. Even if you live alone, you have internal conflict. For example, sometimes I get really annoyed with myself and will actually argue with myself for saying or doing something without thinking. So if it's so easy to get upset at yourself, how can you not get upset with someone else?

Many men and women have told me stories about how conflict led to growth in their lives and relationships.

Ruth, for example, told me that after fifteen years of marriage, she decided she wanted to go to work. Her husband, Matt, agreed that it would probably be a good idea. Once Ruth started working, it quickly became clear that she could not possibly continue to perform all the chores she had when she was at home full time.

However, her husband still expected her to continue running the household and not have his life altered in any way. Ruth said they argued like crazy for six months, until they finally decided that in order for their marriage to work they would have to reach a compromise. They agreed to divide the work evenly, and discovered that besides the housework and other weekend chores, there were several things that had to be done at the end of each day:

- The children had to be picked up at the baby-sitter.
- There was usually some shopping to do, either at the supermarket, department store, or drugstore.
- Dinner had to be prepared and the dishes washed.
- The children, who were too young to do it themselves, had to be bathed.
- The house had to be tidied up.

- The children needed some quality time with their parents before they went to sleep.
- Phone calls needed to be returned to family, friends, and business associates.

They made a list. Each Sunday they reviewed it and divided the chores for the following week. This approach led to a more relaxed, happier relationship. Ruth gained self-esteem, because she enjoyed working and contributing to the family income. When Matt realized how much Ruth had done for the family over the past fifteen years, he gained a deeper appreciation of his wife. He also felt less pressured to earn more money with the additional income from Ruth's job.

If Ruth had tried to be Superwoman in order to avoid arguing, their marriage would have continued to deteriorate and might even have ended in divorce. Instead, having to deal with conflict for several months actually improved their marriage, because it forced them to grow and change.

Frances was an executive secretary who earned an excellent income when she met Frank. Frances had a long-standing desire to get a degree in law. Shortly after they were married, Frances broached the subject of quitting work to attend law school full time, an idea that was not received favorably by Frank. "He complained bitterly about the crimp my not working would put in our finances," said Frances.

"If you don't work, we won't be able to buy that condominium we're so excited about, or take any more expensive vacations!" he yelled at her.

"We argued about it constantly for three months,

before I finally decided that I had to pursue my dream or I would never be happy. Those three months were an absolute nightmare," Frances recalled. "I can honestly say that I graduated from law school *in spite of my husband.* How we stayed married during that time still remains a mystery," she said.

Frances did graduate from law school and now works for a well-known law firm—and Frank is her biggest fan! He loves to boast about his wife, and tells everyone how proud he is that she had the courage of her convictions. Frances's new career has also made it possible for them to enjoy some of the finer things in life, including a beautiful new home and an African safari—one of Frank's lifelong dreams.

Again, this couple's growth would not have been possible if Frances had decided that her goals were less important than keeping the peace. While she might have appeased her husband by staying with an unfulfilling job, her resentment toward him would have created a destructive wall between them that would have prevented the happiness they now enjoy.

When I interviewed Carl, he volunteered that conflict in his marriage definitely had led to growth. "On weekends all I ever wanted to do was relax and watch sports on TV," he told me.

His wife, Tanya, on the other hand, wanted his company on weekends, and insisted he go window-shopping or run errands with her, so that they could be together. After months of arguing, they finally compromised. Carl agreed to go out on Saturday nights with Tanya and go on a family outing on Sunday, if he could relax during the day on Saturday and watch TV.

That conflict led to several improvements in their lives. Tanya learned not to be so dependent on Carl for company, and instead began to make dates with her friends for luncheons and shopping sprees. Carl, on the other hand, looked forward to their date nights alone, and actually became closer to his children as they enjoyed their Sunday adventures.

Marla talked to me about the frustration she had experienced as a result of being the person responsible for paying the bills in her marriage. "My husband's extravagance was ruining our budget, and we argued about it constantly," she said. She finally got fed up, and one night she handed Ted the checkbook and bills and told him, "Here, you pay the bills. If you don't, nobody will, and the bill collector will be knocking on the door. I've had it. I'm just not willing to take the responsibility for this anymore."

Ted took over and Marla remained steadfast in her decision to stay out of it. "The first few months were difficult," she said. "There were late penalties and stacks of unpaid bills, but I ignored the whole thing," she related. "Then, one night, about four months after I quit, Ted came up to me and put his arms around my waist."

"You were so right," he said gently. "I really was spending too much. I've finally caught up on all of our payments, and I'm determined to keep it that way. No more impulsive spending for me," he promised.

Again, Ted's new, responsible behavior was a result of conflict, and this marriage was also improved by it.

A couple who never argues is unlikely to stay together, and if they should, their energy will be spent on resentment and hostility rather than on growth.

OPPOSITES ATTRACT—TRITE BUT TRUE

I have found that people are almost always attracted to someone who possesses traits that are lacking in themselves. For example, if you are spontaneous and love to do things on the spur of the moment, your mate is probably a man who thinks you're crazy when you suddenly say, "Let's go to Palm Springs tomorrow." His reaction will probably be, "Are you nuts? I need time to prepare for a trip, I can't take off just like that!"

If you love people and enjoy nothing more than a party, I know that at home sits a man who hates groups of people and only enjoys quiet, intimate evenings alone with you. If you're a verbal person who enjoys giving a detailed account and cannot possibly say anything in a few words, chances are your man can summarize an entire movie in less than two minutes or recount an event in one sentence.

If you're neat and organized, your man is probably very disorganized, leaves his clothes lying around everywhere, and says, "Relax, will you? My pants will still be there tomorrow and I can pick them up then."

If you're a person who always puts the needs of others before your own, no doubt you're with a man who thinks only of himself and what he wants.

If you're a woman who loves to spend money and buy things, he probably tries to hoard every penny.

The penny-pincher is always attracted to the free-spender.

If you're emotional, he's logical. If you're easygoing and relaxed, he's probably tense and anxious. If you're a clock-watcher who is never late, he's a procrastinator who's never on time.

Now if we analyze why this is true, we'll find that both partners in a couple always complement each another. *Your* strengths are *his* weaknesses, and *his* strengths are *your* weaknesses. It's like two pieces of a puzzle that fit together. Believe me when I tell you that you must appreciate your mate for his characteristics, and that you each have something to learn from the other.

I am an emotional woman married to a logical man. I can't tell you how many times I've exclaimed frantically, "Oh, no! This is terrible. Whatever am I going to do?" Can you imagine what would happen if I were married to someone who got caught up in my hysteria and became equally confused? With my Type A personality, there's no way I could have functioned all these years. Instead, I have a man who calmly says, "Ellen, this is not the end of the world. Let's look at it logically."

I remember going on vacation to San Francisco twenty years ago and leaving all my makeup at home. I was absolutely beside myself, but my husband simply said, "We'll go buy whatever you need at a nearby department store." At the time, I wanted to strangle him, but now, when I pack for a trip I'm not frantic, because I know that if I forget something it's okay. I'm not going to the middle of a jungle where the forgotten item cannot be replaced.

After our twenty-two years of living together, I have become a much more sensible person who is able to solve problems. At the same time, my husband has become much more emotional and sensitive, and doesn't feel he's less of a man if he cries because his son or daughter has received a special award, or a movie is particularly moving.

I'm also the kind of person who wakes up as if from a coma every morning. Like Snoopy, I am truly allergic to mornings. I'm an evening person. I don't even start to come alive until about 10:00 P.M. Most of my writing or reading is done between midnight and 2:00 A.M., when everyone else is asleep. My husband, on the other hand, wakes up cheerful and sings in the shower and is usually exhausted by 11:00 P.M. Not only do I not sing in the morning, I have trouble simply breathing. So here we have what I call a morning person living with an evening person. What is it we've learned from each other? I have experienced the pleasure of a brisk walk in the morning and understand the quiet beauty of nature at dawn, and he has experienced dancing the night away. Every once in a while, one of us goes out of our way to please the other so that we can spend time together enjoying each other's pleasures. But on a routine basis, I don't ask him to stay up with me until two in the morning, and he doesn't poke me at 5:30 A.M.

At the beginning of one of my classes for men, I was approached by a gentleman who said, "I don't know how this class can improve our marriage. If my wife and I are in a building and we both need to get to the top, I'll take the stairs because I love to breathe the air, listen to the sounds, and enjoy the physical effort it takes to get there. My wife will use the elevator. How can two people as different as we are make it?"

My answer to him was, "By the end of this course, I hope you will take the stairs, she will take the elevator, and when you reach the top, you'll have a lovely dinner together and talk about how you both got there. Don't expect her to use the stairs, and you don't have to use the elevator. Try to appreciate that both of you have different ways of getting where you're going and that neither is right or wrong—just different. When you reach that level of thinking, then it would be fantastic if once in a while you took the elevator and she used the stairs, but not on a routine basis."

VIVE LA DIFFÉRENCE!

Another important principle on how to love someone for who they are, not what you want them to be, is to remember that we are all different. Not better or worse, not good or bad, not right or wrong—just different! In fact, it is usually our differences that attract us to each other.

One of my students, Jane, held a Ph.D. and was an executive with a large corporation. At thirty-five, she had never been married, or even been close to marriage. All of sudden she fell madly, passionately in love. One Friday afternoon the entire company where she worked stopped what they were doing and practically hung out the windows in an effort to catch a glimpse of Jane's new boyfriend when he came by to pick her up. The only way I can describe him to you is to say that he was a biker. He drove up on his Harley-Davidson, his long hair blowing in the wind, and Jane, the executive in the three-piece suit, climbed on the back of the motorcycle, wrapped her arms around her "knight" 's waist, and off they rode into the sunset.

Jane asked me if I thought she was crazy, since everyone else thought so. I told her I understood perfectly what made her relationship work. Here is a dedicated, serious, goal-oriented woman who has finally found someone who makes her laugh and enjoy life. Her lover is teaching her how to live one day at a time and not take life so seriously. He's very spontaneous, unconventional, and romantic. She, on the other hand, is providing him with the stability and structure he has been missing. Each comes into the other's life to bring about a balance.

It's wrong to judge another just because his style is different from yours. You cannot say to another person, "Do things my way . . . think exactly the way I think . . . trust whom I trust . . . believe in what I believe in." It is this message that usually destroys the love you first felt. It says, "I loved you in the beginning for who you were, but now I've decided that's no longer good enough. If you want my love, you must change."

If one partner feels he has to sacrifice his identity in a relationship, he doesn't feel loved anymore—he feels used. The secret to keeping love alive is to maintain your uniqueness while increasing intimacy.

Sylvia, another student, came to class one evening in tears. She couldn't stand it anymore. Her husband kept demanding perfection. He had enrolled her in a cooking class so she could learn to be a gourmet cook; an exercise class so she could maintain a perfect heart, lungs, and body; and a time-management class so she could run the household more efficiently. Every morning he'd weigh her, and if she had gained weight, he wouldn't make love to her until she lost the excess pounds. Sylvia had completely lost her sense of self. All she did was try to please her husband. He was a very successful lawyer who had married a vivacious, bubbly, and carefree high school cheerleader. Now the cheerleader was tired and depressed most of the day.

I did my best to help Sylvia understand that she was exactly what he needed, otherwise he wouldn't have fallen in love with her, but she had not been willing to clash with him in order to keep her uniqueness. When her husband enrolled in the men's class, he came to realize that all of the fun and sensuality he had experienced with this woman in the beginning was gone. By learning to examine how she brought balance into his life, he was finally able to encourage her to express her own individuality.

Many women complain that their husbands don't talk. "When we go to a party, all he does is sit and listen," one complained to me. Since I know that opposites attract, I know that this is an outgoing woman who has fallen in love with a self-contained, quiet man. In the beginning, she loved the fact that he was a good listener, always mellow and calm. Now, she takes the very traits she fell in love with and uses them as a weapon against him. Before they leave for a party, she may say something like, "Don't sit there like a bump on a log tonight. Please open your mouth and say something." If she doesn't say this before they leave, she'll probably attack him when they get home.

To understand how unfair this is, imagine what it feels like when the situation is reversed. I'm a very social person, and usually can't wait to get together with a group of people and find out everything about them. If, before we left for a party, my husband said to me, "I don't want you to open your mouth tonight at all. Not one word. Don't ask about anyone's life, how they met, what they do. NOTHING! Keep your mouth closed the entire night," the evening would be complete torture to me. This is exactly how an introverted person feels when told to open his mouth and talk.

If you allow a person the freedom to be himself without labeling his behavior good or bad, right or wrong, he'll want to be the best person possible and give you what you need to make you happy. If everyone had to be strong-willed, outgoing, and charismatic, we wouldn't have any artists, writers, or inventors—people who are often introverted but very gifted. If no one were allowed to be talkative, animated, and expressive, we wouldn't have any actors, salesmen, or teachers in this world. There is just as much value in listening as there is in speaking. Someone who is different from you has just as much value as you do! Remember, if two people agree on everything, then one of them is really not necessary in the relationship.

I'm very happy to have three children who are all very different. I wouldn't want a "Kreidman child"—one stamped from the same mold as all the others.

They all have unique personalities, are sensitive to different things, are motivated in different ways. They will all choose different professions, because all three have different interests. The most important gift I can give them as a parent is belief in themselves and their worth, and to let them know what a difference their existence has made. The most important gift I can give my husband is to love him for who he is, and let him know how grateful I am that he came into my life.

But feeling these things is not enough! They have to be verbalized. Establishing new habits requires action. The following assignment will help you get started and serve as a reminder not to take the love you are sharing for granted. Invest in some index cards, the bigger the better, and use them for this assignment and the ones to come in the following chapters.

ACTION ASSIGNMENT #1

On an index card, write the following:

- **Tell my mate how glad I am that he is part of my life, and how lucky I am to have him.**

Slip your arms around his waist one evening and say, "Honey, I've got to be the luckiest woman alive. I'm so glad you are part of my life. I can't imagine what my life would be like if I hadn't (met) or (married) you."

On another card, write:

- **Tell my mate that I love him just the way he is and that I wouldn't trade him for any other man in the world.**

Again, put your arms around him and tell him, "I really do love you for who you are. I know sometimes we have different views and a different way of doing things, but that's why I fell in love with you.

"You are so exciting to live with, and I get so much out of being with you. I wouldn't trade you for any other man in the whole world."

If he says, "Oh, yeah. What about Tom Selleck?" remember, he's just testing you. Your reply should be, "Are you kidding? He doesn't hold a candle to you. You don't have any competition."

3

SEX OBJECTS—
JUST ONCE IN A WHILE

Sherry came to class because she was tired of living with a grumpy, critical, self-centered man, and was desperate to see if she could do anything to change the situation. "After the second week of class, I returned home feeling 'in love' with my husband for the first time in many years," Sherry told me. "Things got very romantic that night, and afterward my husband lay back on the pillow, sighed, and said, 'Consider me lit!!'

"This came about because I took the advice you had given us, about observing all the wonderful things about our mates and verbalizing them, but I took it to the extreme. I *showered* him with compliments, and right before my eyes I saw Mark go from his usual grumpy self to a man who was cheerful, accepting, and loving," she continued.

"Three weeks into the course, I was thrilled to receive my first romantic letter. I've enclosed the parts of it that are appropriate to share. The rest is too personal and embarrassing, but in a good way."

Here's what Mark wrote:

To the love of my life—

Sherry, I can't believe my ears anymore. I'm not complaining, mind you. I'm thankful. Can it be true? After all these years, I'm falling in love with you all over again. You deserve so much more than I've been giving you. You know my job has been the brunt of my depression, but somehow everything seems bearable now.

With the new excitement I feel for you, I have the strength to finally make some necessary changes. I only hope I can begin to give you what you've given me in the past few weeks. Because of you, I feel alive for the first time in many years.

If I were to ask the average woman how long it's been since she's been complimented on her physical appearance, most would reply, "Just yesterday," or at most, "Just last week." Certainly, not one of them would say, "I haven't received a compliment in more than twenty-five years!" Most men, believe it or not, can't remember the last time they received a compliment on their physical appearance. Even a woman who lives with a man who is not very complimentary will still hear compliments from her children, her friends, and her associates. In my case, there has always been such a great contrast between what I look like when I'm home and what I look like when I'm dressed to go out, that even when my children were very young, they would say, "Oh, Mommy, you look so pretty tonight." My husband, on the other hand, wears a suit to work every day, so the children never really notice if he's dressed up or not, and they have never said, "Oh, Daddy, you look so handsome."

Whenever my husband wears a new suit to work, I ask him if anyone noticed how handsome he looked, and he always says, "No, Ellen, you're the only one." Men don't approach him in the office to tell him how great he looks, and neither do the women—they don't want to seem as if they are "coming on" to him. So the truth is, if he doesn't hear it from me, he isn't going to hear a compliment.

My two teenage girls always get compliments when they wear something new to school. Sometimes even their teachers tell them how nice they look in a particular outfit. In contrast, my son's appearance is usually ignored. No one comments if he wears new pants or a new shirt.

Now anyone who has sons can tell you that teenage boys spend just as much time in front of a mirror—and care just as much about their appearance—as teenage girls do. Yet our society fails to recognize how much the male of the species needs approval of his physical appearance. Little boys often stop hearing how cute they are by the time they are five years old, and some may not get another compliment on their looks for the next forty years!

Most men love to be complimented on their masculinity. How many men "pump iron" till they're exhausted just to develop a body that someone will notice? When you think about it, it's really sad that a man's need to be appreciated for his physical appearance is ignored. Gene, a student in my men's class, told us how awful he felt when he shaved his mustache off and nobody noticed. "I agonized over whether to shave it or not for more than six months before I finally decided to do it," Gene said. "But when I got to the office, no one even noticed."

He paused for a moment, and then said, "No, I take it back. One of the secretaries I've worked with for more than two years told me something looked different about me, and asked if I had gotten a haircut recently. Boy, what a letdown," he concluded.

As women, we find it hard to imagine what it must be like to walk around and be "invisible." It's inconceivable that if a woman made a drastic change in her appearance, such as changing her hair from a shoulder-length style to short and curly, it could be ignored. Yet it happens to men all the time.

Consider how Ben felt on his wedding day. "I really envied my bride," he told the other men in class. "Everyone at the reception came up and told Marci how beautiful she looked, and how lovely her dress was. I kept waiting for someone to notice me, but no one did," he remembers sadly.

"I had gone to a hairstylist, instead of a barber, for the first time in my life. I had rented a great-looking tuxedo, and I had spent hours getting ready. I wanted to look good too—after all, it was my wedding also! It sure would have been nice if someone had noticed."

Jim Sanderson, whose column "The Liberated Male" appears in the *Los Angeles Times,* wrote about this subject in an article titled "Viewing Men as Sex Objects."

> Every woman resents the way males constantly focus on her body. Every woman would like to be admired for her mind and her talent too—for what she can do and not just what she is. It's just the reverse for a male. We're tired of praise for what we can do; we'd all just love to be sex objects once in a while. Women say they hate to be ogled by construction workers, but I tell you if the girls in the beauty salon want to lean out the door and whistle as I walk by, well hell, ladies, what time would be convenient for you?

When a man is given a compliment, he tends to respond quickly. For example, one Monday morning Pat, an outgoing person anyway, passed her coworker Tom in the hallway at work and smiled at him. On Tuesday, when she saw him again, she said, "That suit you have on looks really great. Navy blue is definitely your color."

Tom thanked her and continued on his way. Later that afternoon, Pat's phone rang, and there on the other end of the line was the man in the navy-blue suit—asking if she was free for lunch on Wednesday! "I couldn't believe my ears," Pat said. "All I did was pay him a compliment."

Justine decided to put her newfound knowledge about complimenting men into action. The weekend after her class, she and a few close friends checked into a local resort. They spent the afternoon on the beach, and a few blankets away she noticed a man chatting with a group of friends. She couldn't take her eyes off his beautiful smile. Her heart started to race as she thought, How am I going to tell him what I'm thinking? I'm twenty-eight years old, and I've never done this type of thing before. I'm so embarrassed!

Gathering her courage, she sauntered down the beach and as she passed his blanket she blurted out, "I don't know if anyone has ever told you this before, but you have a fantastic smile." She continued walking, and before she knew it, he was at her side. "Hey," he said, "you can't just keep on walking after a compliment like that! I want to meet you." They began walking together and ended up getting something to drink. That afternoon he asked her for a date, and she told the class, "We've been inseparable ever since."

Bess came to class one week beaming. She had been working for more than three years as a secretary at the same company. A new salesman had caught her eye months ago, but he didn't even know she existed. "I decided to do something about it," Bess said.

"I summoned every ounce of courage I had, thinking, What have I got to lose, and the next time he gave me a contract to type, I looked up and said, "Hey, hotshot. You're really something. I guess when you combine your good looks and your ability, it all adds up to being a winner. There's not another salesman in this office who has gotten as many sales as you have. I hope your boss appreciates you and knows what a contribution you are making to this company."

The salesman stood there a moment, not saying anything, but she could see the gleam in his eye. Then, quite suddenly, he said that any woman who could make him feel that good deserved dinner, and he asked her if she was busy that night. "We've been together seven days straight," Bess said.

One of my students told the class that she had never been attracted to her husband's body—only his mind. She described him as a brilliant and very successful man who owned his own company. "Physically," Joan said, "he is very skinny and his body is covered with hair from his neck to his toes. Naked, he looks like a skinny, scrawny monkey."

After a vacation in Tahiti, her husband was showing pictures of their vacation at the office. In many pictures, he was wearing either shorts or a bathing suit, with his body exposed. When one of his young secretaries saw the pictures, she exclaimed, "I didn't know you had such a gorgeous hairy chest! That really turns me on." When he came home that night, he couldn't wait to tell his wife what his secretary had said. Joan just rolled her eyes and continued talking about something else.

A few months later, Joan and her husband attended a going-away party for one of her husband's coworkers. Everyone had had a little too much to drink, and the same young secretary stepped up to Joan's husband, unbuttoned his shirt, and caressed his chest, saying, "All I can think about when I see you is that gorgeous hairy chest of yours." As he stood there grinning from ear to ear, Joan glowered at him and said, "That's it, we're leaving!" His reply, of course, was, "Why are you ruining the best evening I've ever had?"

The reason I tell you this story is that most of us never know what we've been missing until someone gives something to us that we've never experienced before. Since most men aren't accustomed to hearing compliments about their bodies, they don't know what they're missing. Believe me when I tell you that the first time a woman tells him what gorgeous sexy eyes he has, or compliments him on his strong legs, he's gone! Although they are unaware of it, most men are starving for this kind of attention. I can't tell you how frustrated I feel every time a woman in my class tells me that her husband has started running or working out with weights and when he asks if she can see any difference, she responds, "No, not really." How utterly depressing!

NOTICE YOUR MAN

- Notice his muscular legs.
- Notice his masculine chest.
- Notice his handsome face.
- Notice his gorgeous head of hair.
- Notice his sexy eyes.
- Notice his beautiful smile.
- Notice his broad shoulders.
- Notice his large, masculine hands.
- Notice his deep voice.
- Notice anything that makes him a male.

Another way to let him know you appreciate his physical appearance is to compare him to the leading character in a movie. Marie, a student in her early fifties, was so inspired by one of my classes that one evening she went home and, while her husband slept, she wrote "You Tarzan. Me Jane. Let's swing tonight" across the bathroom mirror in deep red lipstick. When her husband got up the next morning and started shaving, he made no comment. As she pretended to be asleep, Marie thought, You son of a gun. Why aren't you reacting?

"It wasn't like I had written it in a corner," she told the class. "This was across the whole mirror in bold red lipstick."

Her husband left for work, still saying nothing. But at eleven-thirty that morning, the telephone rang. Her husband was on the phone, saying, "I can't stand it anymore. Did you really mean what you wrote on the mirror?"

His wife said, "I sure did. You're my Tarzan!"

He was home from work by noon, and for the first time in thirty years they made love in the middle of the day!

Another one of my students told us that the night she called her boyfriend and said she couldn't wait to see her "Rambo," he proposed to her. In the article I've already quoted, Jim Sanderson said that one night a woman who was observing him disrobe murmured, "Oh, at last I know what Michelangelo meant," when she saw his body!

Another student, Marlene, confided in the class that before she made love to her husband she always said, "Come here, my Rocky."

All of these expressions make a man feel more masculine—one of the most wonderful feelings he can have. He may be praised for his accomplishments all day long, but knowing that you think he is sexy and that you appreciate him for his physical characteristics makes him feel very special.

We'll talk specifically about lovemaking in Chapter 5, but it is important that you understand that most men feel insecure about themselves as lovers. They want desperately to please you, and when they get no feedback, they interpret it as a negative reaction. Many women have told me, "I *never* say anything negative. I don't say anything at all."

Well, what if you wore a new dress or changed your hairdo and your best friend said nothing? Would you interpret that in a positive way? Of course not! No comment is generally taken to mean dissatisfaction or displeasure.

The next time you make love, tell your man what a wonderful lover he is and how much pleasure he gives you. Tell him he's a real stud and how lucky you feel to have a man who is great in bed. I'll talk more about this in Chapter 5, "Romance Is a Decision."

WE ALL WANT TO MATTER

One of the most rewarding feelings we can have comes from affecting someone's life in a positive way. For most people, there is no greater joy than knowing that you brought another person more happiness, fulfillment, insight, or knowledge. In other words, because of you the quality of someone else's life improved. In contrast, finding out that we affected someone else's life in a negative way is a terrible feeling.

We all want to matter in a positive way, but rather than not matter at all, we often choose to matter in a negative way.

This is why people have marital problems, relationship problems, and discipline problems. When our family members act badly, they are saying to us, "Look, I really want to matter to you. If I can't matter in a positive way, then rather than not matter at all, I'll matter in a negative way."

A wife who feels her husband is ignoring her or not spending enough time with her will subconsciously think, Oh, yeah? You think you can ignore me, that I don't matter? You don't even know I'm alive! Well I'll show you, buddy! I'm going to start an argument, because even feeling angry is better than feeling nothing at all!

Leona said she verges on being a compulsive shopper to make up for the lack of time her husband spends with her. She said, "I guess at a subconscious level, I'm getting back at him for not paying enough attention to me. Robert is a busy executive and is gone much of the time. Even though money isn't a problem, I do go overboard just to get him angry. When he starts yelling about the bills at the end of the month, at least he's paying some sort of attention, even if it's negative attention."

In the men's class, Todd admitted that he flirts with other women just to make his wife jealous. "She's so involved with the kids and volunteering her time to everyone but me, I figure that if she thinks I'm interested in other women, she may start paying attention to me. When she's jealous, she usually starts slamming cabinet doors, and huffs and puffs around the house. I know it sounds weird, but it's then that I feel like I matter to her."

Another man, Harold, spends more time at the office than necessary because it's the only place he feels important. "When I do go home," he told the class, "there is always a lot of chaos. My wife runs a home-based business, and there's almost always someone there when I get home," he complained. "Other times, I get home and she's gone to a class of some kind or to another meeting. It's as if she's afraid to spend any time with me alone," he continued.

"At work I get lots of strokes and people think I'm doing a great job. Why should I bother to be where I don't feel very good about myself?" he asked.

A man who comes home and finds his mate on the telephone may feel neglected or unimportant, but instead of saying so directly, he'll choose to start an argument over something unrelated. If you compare the feelings of the man who is ignored with the feelings of a man who is greeted with, "Oh, I'm so glad you're home, I missed you so much," you can see how the second man will feel as if he matters and will be in a good mood.

THE BEST-KEPT SECRET ABOUT MEN

A woman who knows that inside every man, no matter how old, how successful, or how powerful, there is a little boy who wants to be loved and to feel as if

he's special is a woman who knows a powerful secret. A man wants to know that he matters to you
more than anyone else in the world. He wants to matter to you more than your parents, more than your
children, more than your friends, and more than your
job.

If he could verbalize it, a man would say, "Tell me
why I make a difference. Tell me why I matter to you.
Tell me over and over again. Don't tell me just once.
Tell me every day of my life. Keep complimenting me
and recognize my strengths. I want to be your knight
in shining armor. I want to be your hero."

Men tend to fulfill our expectations of them and to
become what they hear continually reinforced. The
way to get positive behavior is to reinforce positive
behavior constantly. The German author Goethe said:

"If you treat a man as he is, he'll stay as he is, but if
you treat him as if he were what he ought to be, and
could be, he will become the bigger and better man."

My husband constantly hears what a wonderful
husband and father he is, which makes him want to
be an even better father and husband.

It's a rare woman whose husband will go shopping
with her for clothes. Today, Wilma is one of those
women, but it wasn't always so. Recently, Wilma had
a formal dinner to go to. After hearing my advice, she
approached her husband to say, "You have such great
taste and always know what looks best on me. I really
value your opinion and would very much appreciate
it if you would help me select a dress for next Friday
evening." She couldn't believe it when he smiled and
said he'd go shopping with her.

Beth's husband is one who willingly fixes things

around the house—now! Before she took my class, however, Beth had been in the habit of referring to her husband as lazy and incapable. After Light His Fire, Beth decided to try a new approach. When she wanted to have her kitchen wallpapered, she put her arms around Hal and said, "I stopped at the wall-paper store today. The salesman there told me how difficult it is to wallpaper if you've never done it before.

"I'll bet if you wanted to, you could do a great job. You have such a great eye for detail and could match up patterns easily."

Hal beamed and said, "You're probably right. Okay, when do you want me to take on this project?"

When you let a man know you value an ability or strength that he doesn't even know he possesses, he wants to prove you right.

Another student is now living in the house of her dreams because of her husband's creative financing. She explained that they returned home depressed after looking for new homes. Don immediately turned on the TV to escape, while Patti put the knowledge she had gained in my class into action. Cuddling up next to him, she said, "Honey, you're a math whiz. I'll bet if you worked with the numbers a bit, you'd come up with an ingenious idea."

Much to Patti's amazement, Don turned off the TV, got out a pencil and paper, and spent the next few hours figuring out how they could swing the deal.

Rebecca now owns her own business, thanks to her husband's help in putting together a detailed busi-ness plan to attract investors. "When I realized I'd be under-capitalized, I knew I needed to get other people to invest in my business, but when I learned how much it would cost to have it done by a professional, I went to my husband.

"You're the smartest man I know. You know more about business and financing than anyone else out there. I know you could come up with a better business plan than any professional could, and it could save me anywhere from three thousand to six thousand dollars," Rebecca told her husband.

These women all know that you can catch more flies with honey than you can with vinegar.

Instead of being critical, start to notice your mate's positive traits. Notice what is wonderful and good about him. Find at least one thing to compliment him on every day, no matter how small. Even something as simple as telling him you love his smile, or that every time he walks into the room he makes it brighter, besides making him feel good and look forward to coming home, will make him want to please you.

Most of our men come from environments with varying degrees of positive reinforcement. A man who grew up with very few compliments will need double the dose, and anyone who brags, boast, or stretches the truth needs three times the praise that an ordinary person does. Remember this rule:

The more I like myself, the less I have to impress or convince you how great I am. The less I like myself, the more I have to convince people how wonderful I am. The degree to which I either like or dislike myself has a great deal to do with how much or how little praise I received as a child.

If your mate was deprived of praise as a child, be

prepared to give him *all* that he's been missing. I mean, I want you to "pour it on" so thick that anyone else would think you'd gone mad! What you'll find is that it is not too thick and it's not too much. It is never, ever "too much" to appreciate, praise, and compliment another human being.

I'm assuming that by now you have had an opportunity to practice my advice at the beginning of this chapter on making your mate feel like a "sex object." Now, you are going to appreciate him, not only for his physical characteristics, but for everything he does, says, and stands for. That may sound like a lot, but remember you want to Light His Fire, and this is one of the ways to do it.

COMPLIMENT HIM FOR THE THINGS HE DOES:

- **If he washes the car—**
  Tell him how much you appreciate the pride he takes in keeping the car clean.
- **If he fixes the car—**
  Tell him how lucky you are to have someone with so much mechanical ability.
- **If he fixes things around the house—**
  Sing, "It's so nice to have a man around the house."
- **If he exercises—**
  Tell him how wonderful it is to have a man who is in great shape and takes pride in his body.
- **If he's taking classes—**
  Tell him you love his quest for knowledge.

- **If he's on any volunteer committees—**
  Tell him how wonderful he is to give his time to causes.
- **If he plays with the children—**
  Tell him how lucky the children are to have a father like him.
- **If he plays with the dog—**
  Tell him how terrific it is to have a strong man who also has a tender side.
- **If he earns a great deal of money—**
  Tell him you never dreamed you'd have the lifestyle he has provided for you.

COMPLIMENT HIM ON THE THINGS HE SAYS:

- **If he's funny—**
  Tell him you love his sense of humor and how great it makes you feel.
- **If he's complimentary—**
  Tell him how lucky you are to have a man who notices.
- **If he's always dreaming—**
  Tell him you love him because he is goal-oriented and thinking of the future.
- **If he solves a problem—**
  Tell him how much his logic improves the quality of your life.
- **If he's very verbal—**
  Tell him he's the "life of the party," how much you love to listen to him, and how he always makes people feel at ease.

- **If he's nonverbal—**
  Tell him what a good listener he is, and what a calming influence he has on you.

COMPLIMENT HIM FOR THE THINGS HE STANDS FOR:

- **If he's honest—**
  Tell him how much you love that quality.
- **If he's loyal—**
  Tell him how wonderful it is to be able to trust him.
- **If he's dependable—**
  Tell him how secure you feel being with someone you can always depend on.
- **If he's a risk-taker—**
  Tell him you love his courage to stand behind what he believes in.
- **If he's confident—**
  Tell him that his belief in himself makes you believe in him.

I hope by now you've got the idea. Everything and anything should be noticed and commented on in a positive way—with a compliment.

BE AN ACTRESS

What if you tend to be a negative person and you're saying, "I can't possibly do this, it's just *not me*"? Well then, don't be you. Be someone else! Make believe you're a positive person who easily notices everything wonderful about your man.

In business we are told to "dress for success" and in sales there is a phrase that says, "Act the part and you shall be the part." For example, when you go to work in real estate sales, you are advised to get yourself a good suit, an expensive pair of shoes, and a late-model car in order to appear successful, because no one is going to buy or list a house with you if they think it's your first sale. "Act as if" you are successful, and eventually you will be. What is pretense in the beginning becomes real.

I remember reading an interview with Cary Grant, in which he was asked how he became the suave, debonair man that every woman found irresistible. He answered that he had been an awkward, gangly teenager who used to make believe he was wonderful, suave, and debonair. Soon he was unable to tell the difference between his make-believe self and his real self.

GIVE THE PEOPLE YOU LOVE THE MOST

We lie to strangers all the time because we don't want to hurt their feelings. For instance, if I were to come into your home and spill coffee all over your new couch I'd be very upset and you'd probably calm me down and tell me not to worry about it. But if a member of your family did the same thing, I wouldn't want to be there to hear you scream at him for his stupidity.

When we start a new job and the boss asks how it's

going, most of us grin and say, "Fine." We wouldn't dream of telling him how overwhelmed we feel or how afraid we are that we'll never learn it all. We'd save the truth until we got home, and then we'd dump it on the people we love.

If a friend came to us crying because of the awful haircut and perm she just got, almost all of us would say, "It's really not bad. In fact, it's kind of cute once you get used to it."

Even though we may not feel like it, we all smile pleasantly and greet people whom we can't stand but are forced to work with. Why can't we do the same thing with the people we love? Why can't we say something complimentary and enjoy the feeling of giving someone else pleasure, even when we're really feeling rather neutral?

I'm suggesting that we learn to give the people we love the most, what we somehow give instinctively to strangers and acquaintances. Initially, most women in my class say, "Oh, I can't say anything nice unless I mean it." But when they stop to think about it, they realize that they say things they don't mean to strangers all day long. Why not give the same gift to those you love? According to *Funk & Wagnalls Standard Dictionary*, to *appreciate* means to increase in value. Increase the value of your lover by giving him praise, compliments, and appreciation.

An ad in the personals of a New York paper read: I am 32, 6 feet tall, handsome, well built, athletic, intelligent, absolutely amazing and completely perfect in every way. I'd like to meet a woman who'll humor me when I get like this.

Although the ad is written in a humorous style, I

sense that inside that man, and every man, is a desire for his mate to see him as having all the qualities he wishes he had. Remember, your love, to some degree, is a measure of his worth. Become a woman who is indispensable to your man and his self-image, and you will be a woman to whom a man feels deeply committed.

ACTION ASSIGNMENT #2

Take out another index card and write on it:

> Make sure that once a day
> I give my love a compliment.
> Compliment what he does,
> What he says, or what he stands for.
> Tell him how much he matters to me.

On the same card, make a list of some of the famous characters who have been especially masculine. Find opportunities to compare your mate to these characters, saying something like, "Oh, honey, you're as strong as the Incredible Hulk," after he does something that requires masculine strength.

Other examples are:

1. Tarzan
2. King Kong
3. Rocky
4. Rambo
5. Superman

6. Casanova
7. Adonis
8. Latin lover (if it applies. On second thought, even if it doesn't apply!)

4

COMMUNICATION

When Amelia first came to class, she couldn't understand why she never had more than a first date with a man. "I'm intelligent, young, and successful in the business world," she said to me. "I don't understand what's wrong with me. What are men looking for, anyway?" she asked.

It wasn't long before she realized her problem.

"I was doing all of the talking," she confessed to the class after a few weeks. "I wanted to impress my date with all of my accomplishments and attributes. I wanted him to know how lucky he was to be going out with me."

She started dating Ben while she was still attending class, and about six months later she wrote to tell me that she could now look back and see how foolish she had been.

"It's great to have the information you gave while I am young enough to use it," she wrote. Enclosed was the following excerpt from a note sent to her by her new lover:

> . . . you are the most fantastic woman alive. I've never felt this close to anyone before. It seems like I can tell you anything and you always understand and are always there for me.
>
> Sometimes I wonder if there are any other men who are as lucky as I am. Not only are you my lover, you are my best friend. Now that I've found you, I cannot imagine living without you.
>
> Your lover and best friend,
Ben

Taking a vow of silence is not part of the wedding ceremony, so why is it that so many couples stop communicating once they are married? The answer really isn't as complicated as some would have us believe. Let me try to simplify it for you.

Ninety-nine percent of the time, people don't want your advice, your evaluation, your opinion, your critique, or your solution to their problems. They just want you to listen and understand their feelings. Remember I said in the last chapter that we all want to matter? Well, in order for us to know we matter, we must have our feelings validated by someone who knows how to listen effectively.

LISTEN WITH YOUR HEART

Listening correctly is truly an art, but one that can be
learned. In order to listen correctly, you must stop
thinking about your response and concentrate instead on understanding what the other person is saying and feeling. How do you usually react when your
mate comes home and shares an experience he had
that day? I remember when we were first married,
my husband would come home from work and tell
me, for example, how he "blew" a ten-thousand-dol-
lar deal. I'd sit and listen attentively and then offer
him possible solutions. I'd say something like,
"Maybe you didn't blow it. Maybe one more phone
call would do the trick, or maybe you could present
them with an alternative," to which he would angrily
respond, "If you think you can do it better, why don't
you take over my job?" Then I'd get angry back and
start yelling, "Here I am, listening to you and interested in trying to help you, and all I get is yelled at."

Now, I understand that he didn't want me to offer
him a solution. All he wanted was for me to understand what it felt like to fail at getting something he
really wanted and deserved. These days, when a similar situation occurs, my reaction is, "You poor thing. I
feel so bad. It must be awful to work so hard and be
so dedicated and then have the client choose a com-
petitor."

How many times has your mate shared something
with you, and instead of validating him, you sup-
ported the other person? For example, he comes
home and tells you he didn't get the promotion he'd
been hoping for. You proceed to tell him:

1. How lucky he is because he probably wouldn't have been happy in that position anyway; or,
2. His boss must have a good reason for not promoting him; or,
3. The guy that got the promotion has been with the company much longer; or,
4. Now maybe he'll quit this dumb company.

Responding in any of these ways clearly demonstrates that you do not understand how he feels. He's disappointed. His expectations were not met. Your reaction should have been, "How awful! You must be so disappointed. You've worked so hard. That company just doesn't know how lucky they are to have you." Don't offer a solution. Don't offer advice.

Every time my husband comes to me to relate something, I literally say to myself, "Ellen, shut up! He isn't asking for your advice. He just wants you to listen and be there for him."

This was a revelation to my student Diana, whose husband, Ted, and she were not speaking. Ted had complained that his best friend, John, hadn't called in over four months. Diana's response was, "Look, John is a very busy person. He's probably away on business. Why don't you just keep calling him? You don't have to keep track of who called last."

Diana didn't realize that she was defending John instead of seeing the situation through her husband's eyes. She could have said instead, "That is very thoughtless of him. You probably miss talking to him."

You're probably not even aware of how often you

defend a stranger's position rather than see things through the eyes of your loved one.

One of my students, Nadine, was hurt and puzzled when her husband, Patrick, asked her to stop coming to watch him play baseball on Saturday mornings with the company-sponsored team.

"Just don't come anymore, okay? You're always telling me how to play, and you don't even know anything about baseball. Maybe you should play next week, instead of me, so everyone can see what a great job you'd do."

"What did I do wrong?" Nadine asked me in class.

With a little questioning, I was able to get Nadine to admit that in an attempt to be helpful, she ended up sounding critical. "Whenever Patrick's team lost a game, he'd get very angry. I hated to see him so upset, so I'd try to make him feel better," she said.

When I asked her how she did that, she responded, "Well, I gave him advice."

What sort of advice? Below are a few of Nadine's suggestions:

1. You swing too early. You should have waited a little longer.
2. Maybe you should practice more.
3. Did you ever think about taking up another sport, like bowling, that wouldn't be as frustrating?
4. It's not like you're getting paid for this. It's supposed to be fun. Don't take it so seriously.

As Nadine looked at her "constructive criticism" from her husband's point of view, it was easy for her to see why he didn't want her to come to the games any-more. She determined to change her way of relating and see if it would make a difference.

The following week, when Patrick returned home from his game, Nadine could see from his face that it hadn't gone well, but she asked anyway. "Hi, honey," she greeted him. "How was the game?"

"DON'T ASK!" Patrick responded angrily, as he threw his equipment on the floor.

Nadine put her arms around him and said, "Poor baby. I'm sorry you've had such a bad morning, but I've got your favorite lunch ready. Let's eat."

Nadine kept quiet as they ate, saying over and over to herself, "Nadine, be still. He's not asking for advice, criticism, or evaluation. He just wants you to under-stand how he feels."

To her amazement, little by little Patrick started tell-ing her about the game, and when they were finished eating, he sighed a big sigh and said, "Thanks for lunch. I feel better now that I've eaten. Thanks for listening, too. Maybe we'll play better next week!"

YOU CAN'T FIX IT

If you're anything like me, you'll understand when I say I always want to make things better—to "fix it." I always want to prevent pain, hurt, and disappoint-ment, but I can't. Since most of my husband's frustra-tions have to do with his work, I can't make them go away. All I can do is be there for him so he can tell me about his pain, and then validate that what he's feel-ing is okay.

That's why I think that the best therapy is being in a group of people who have experienced situations similar to those that you have been through. For example, I've never had my house robbed, so I can only imagine what such an experience might be like for someone who has. Most people will tell a robbery victim how lucky he is not to have been there while the robbery took place, or that he should be grateful that nothing of value was taken. But if the robbery victim were with a group of people who had all had their houses robbed, they could validate that his anger and frustration had nothing to do with what was taken. His feelings are about the invasion of privacy. One person in the group might reveal how frightened he is every time he puts his key in the lock, even though the police assure him that burglars never return to the same place. Another might confess that even though he now has an alarm system, he's still frightened. Someone else might have moved because he couldn't stand the constant reminder of that awful night he came home to a house that had been ransacked by strangers. But none of them would attempt to offer an answer or a remedy. They would simply share their feelings, and the victim would feel better knowing that he was not alone—that what he was feeling had been felt by others.

When someone loses his job, it doesn't help him a bit when people say, "Oh, don't worry. With your knowledge and ability, you'll find another one soon." Or, "It's the best thing that could have happened to you. You'll see. One door closes, and another one opens." No one acknowledges his fear of not being able to find another job—and the pain such failure would bring.

We've all heard the expression, "I cried because I had no shoes until I met a man who had no feet," but I really don't think hearing that makes anyone feel better in a crisis. Besides, it's absolutely ludicrous to think we can assign a value to whose loss, or tragedy, or disappointment is worse.

When Marie had a miscarriage, she was terribly annoyed by the seemingly endless numbers of people who told her how lucky she was that it happened so early in her pregnancy, or that it was better to miscarry than to give birth to an abnormal child. None of that made her feel better.

"I would have given anything just to have someone say, 'Oh, I'm so sorry. You must feel terrible. What a tragedy. What a loss,' " Marie told me later.

"It didn't help to hear that I'd get over it, or that I would be pregnant again in no time. It's true, I did become pregnant again, but at the time, I just wanted someone to understand what I was feeling."

Marie ended by saying, "It was even worse when people would discount my loss, saying, 'Let me tell you about so and so,' and then recount a story they felt was even sadder than mine."

THE BEST THERAPY MONEY CAN BUY

Psychiatrists get paid lots of money because they know how to acknowledge their patients' feelings. For example, a psychiatrist in one of my classes for men told us his role is to allow people to express themselves and let them know he understands by telling them how they must have felt at the time. He also keeps a box of tissues handy, which they can use anytime. His patients need him to understand what they are going through and to validate their feelings, because they have no one else in their lives to do that for them. If we—as parents, friends, or partners—would do this for each other, fewer people would need to seek professional help.

In the film *Crocodile Dundee,* Dundee can't understand why people in America take their problems to a stranger (a psychiatrist, for example) because in Australia the place to share your problems and get someone to listen to you is at the local pub.

Serena, a beautiful woman whose heart had been broken when her fiancé broke their engagement shortly before their wedding because he had fallen in love with another woman, told the class how she felt about the reaction of her friends and family.

"I got to the point where I wanted to punch out the next person who told me how grateful I should feel that I found out in time," Serena confessed, as she related the various platitudes thrown at her by friends and family.

"I guess people thought they were comforting me when they said things like, 'We knew he wasn't right for you all along,' or 'I've heard she's not nearly as pretty or smart as you. They'll probably be miserable together.' "

Serena told us she ended up in a psychiatrist's office, because she desperately needed someone to validate her feelings—someone who would recognize how awful it felt to have all of her dreams shattered—

to sympathize with her feelings of abandonment, to let her express her anger at being jilted, her embarrassment at having to cancel the plans and call the guests to tell them the wedding was off, and her disappointment at missing out on a honeymoon to Hawaii.

It's not necessary to agree with someone in order to help them; just try to understand what they are feeling. Be sensitive to the fact that we all have certain fears, and that men are no exception. Some men have a fear of aging, for example, or of no longer being physically attractive, while others may fear impotence, not earning enough money, or some other inadequacy. If your man is brave enough to take a chance and voice some of his fears, listen to him and try to sympathize. Assure your man that you believe in him and are always on his side. Let him know that he can always tell you everything. Don't judge—just listen. None of us has the right to judge another until we've walked in his shoes.

When I'm asked by women where they should send their mate for help, I reply, "You try to help him. You be there for him." It's the best therapy money can buy.

When we hear that a friend has suffered a tragedy or a loss, we wonder what we can say to make our friend feel better. Do you know what the answer is? Nothing! Nothing you can say can make him feel better. All you can do is be there for him.

Recently, one of my students lost her husband in a tragic automobile accident. At the funeral, her father-in-law's best friend tried to comfort him by saying, "Fred, be thankful you have five other kids. What would you do if this had been your only child?" Now, this man didn't leave his house saying, "How can I upset my friend?" He left saying, "What can I say to make him feel better?" How much more comforting it would have been if he had just put his arms around his friend and said, "I'm so sorry. I feel so bad. You must be going through hell. I'm here if you need me for anything. Is there anything I can do for you?" His friend probably would have answered, "No, just having you here is a comfort." You don't have to be brilliant or have all the answers in order to be helpful. In fact, you don't have to be smart at all. All you have to do is develop the art of listening and let the other person know you understand what he is feeling and that you are there for him.

The "hug doctor," Leo Buscaglia, wrote an article about children who have made a difference in someone's life. In it, he tells the story of a neighbor whose wife had just died. One of the neighborhood children paid the man a visit and was there for some time. When he returned home, the little boy's mother, believing her son had been bothering the man, asked, "What did you say to Mr. Johnson?" The little boy answered, "I didn't say anything. I just helped him cry." Children instinctively seem to know simply how to *be* with another person and not *do* anything.

There is an ancient proverb that says, "God gave us two ears and only one mouth, which means we are supposed to listen twice as much as we are supposed to talk; otherwise we would have been given two mouths and one ear."

REPLACE A PET WITH A PERSON

Did you know that human beings die if they aren't touched? Well, they do! A study conducted during World War II revealed that the babies in our sterilized American orphanages were dying, while the babies in dirty, unsanitary Mexican orphanages were surviving. When a reason was sought, they discovered that in our orphanages the babies were placed in their cribs in such a way that they could feed on a propped bottle, and the only time the babies were touched was when their diapers were changed. In the Mexican orphanages, on the other hand, each child was assigned a "mama" who would hold, feed, and be with the child. Animals can survive without being touched, but people are often damaged by a lack of touching. In a study conducted years ago, it was observed that most of the criminals on death row had not been touched as children.

We have become a society devoted to stroking and pampering our pets instead of each other. After reading this section, I want you to spend the next week touching your mate instead of your mutt. I believe that many couples, after a certain period of time, experience skin hunger. Remember I said that opposites attract? That means that if one of you is a toucher, chances are the other is not. Usually, the toucher will tell me, "I used to touch my mate all the time, but it embarrassed him so much he asked me not to, so I just stopped."

She shouldn't have stopped! Touching is healthy, and the toucher has a strength the other partner lacks. She should have said instead, "No, I'm not going to stop touching you. I'm going to keep this up for the rest of your life, so you'd better get used to it."

In an article appearing in *New Woman* magazine, entitled "The Art of Hugging," Jim Lytle explains that being hugged causes our body to release endorphins. Known as nature's uppers, these are the chemicals our body releases when we feel great. If you learned that you just won a million dollars in the lottery, for example, you'd release endorphins. Endorphins increase your resistance to disease and help diminish pain. So you see, there is a great deal of healing that occurs when we touch another human being.

Two hundred hospital patients were studied recently to test their response to being touched. Half of the patients were to be touched by every staff member who walked into the room, including doctors, nurses, aides, and even the dietician. The doctor might touch the patient's arm as he asked how the patient was feeling, or a nurse might stroke the patient's hair or shoulder as she gave the medication, and so forth. The other half of the patients were not to be touched at all, except as necessary to perform routine tasks. Amazingly, the patients who were touched healed three times as fast as the ones who weren't touched. As a result of that study, courses called "The Healing Touch" are now offered to nurses.

One of the saddest things about getting older is that the elderly, especially those in convalescent homes, get so few opportunities to touch and be touched. Every year there is a hug booth at the local county fair. Initially, I questioned the appeal of this booth, wondering who would stand in line to be hugged by a stranger. Surprisingly, the hug booth is always the most crowded booth at the fair, with elderly people waiting in line to get their free hugs.

One couple who took my class, owners of a convalescent home, told me that the patients in their home lived for Sundays, when the couple's four-year-old granddaughter came to visit. She would sit on everybody's lap and give all the patients a hug and a kiss, and by Thursday of each week the patients would anxiously start asking if Heather was coming on the following Sunday. Wouldn't it be wonderful if all the children in the community who weren't being touched could visit the retirement homes where the older people are literally dying to touch and be touched?

My husband told me about a management film he saw that demonstrated the power of touching. In the film, as people left a phone booth, they were stopped and asked for directions to a major street in the area. A few minutes later, they were stopped again by someone else, who inquired if they remembered being asked directions, whether it had been a male or female, and if they could describe what he or she was wearing. As the subjects struggled to remember, the camera focused on their embarrassed faces. The few who were able to remember if it had been a male or a female typically had no idea what they had been wearing. The experiment was then repeated with a different group of people, but with one difference. As the questioners asked for directions, they put their hand on the other person's shoulder. These people, when stopped a few minutes later, not only knew whether it had been a man or a woman who had asked for directions, they could actually describe what he or she had been wearing. Obviously, we make a connection when we touch another human being.

REACH OUT AND TOUCH SOMEONE

I've had saleswomen in my classes who have exceeded $1 million a year in sales tell me they have an edge on their male counterparts because they are able to use their femininity. By substituting the masculine handshake for a hug, they always get the sale or increase their business. A group of managers I taught who were involved in direct sales were able to increase their home-party bookings by 50 percent just by touching the guests as they asked if they were interested in hosting the next party.

As we discussed touching in one of my classes, Jean, a real estate agent in her sixties, suddenly realized why her clients were so loyal to her. Most realtors will tell you that clients are not loyal. They'll list their property with you for a short time, and if they don't get results, they'll change to another company. A couple searching for a home will look with a variety of agents. Jean never experienced such disloyalty—not because, as her office coworkers believed, she was a grandmother figure—but because, as she said, "I'm a toucher. I can't keep my hands off people, and once we work together, they feel like I'm part of their family."

Paula, a single parent in her forties raising three children, was so motivated after the lecture on touching that she went home and made it a point to hug each of her teenagers. As a result, they followed her around that evening like puppy dogs, talking non-stop. They even stood outside the door and talked to her while she was in the bathroom. Usually, she and her kids just greeted each other with a routine, "Hi, how was your day?" with no one bothering to answer or listen. But this night they all wound up on her bed talking, and it was 2:00 A.M. before everyone finally went to sleep. It was like one big pajama party. Paula said it had been years since they had all felt so close. Reach out and touch someone!

Here's a little game you can play with your mate. The next time you go to a party or gathering, tell him he has to touch you three times during the evening and that you'll do the same. It can be any kind of contact—a kiss, a pat on the back, a squeeze of the hand—as long as it connects you.

After hearing me describe this game in class, one of my students, Bonnie, decided to try it on her husband, Mel. One evening, just as they were leaving the house to attend an awards banquet, Bonnie told Mel about the game. She suggested that they should connect at least six times during the evening, preferably with a kiss. Mel, who never displays affection in public, objected vigorously. "That's ridiculous," he said. "I'd be much too embarrassed."

Nevertheless, Bonnie persisted. "We can do this very discreetly," she told Mel. "Unless, of course, you prefer it to be a full-blown scene, with me throwing my arms around you and kissing you passionately," she teased him.

Reluctantly, Mel agreed, with a trace of a grin.

"It was a lot of fun," Bonnie told the class the following week. "We sneaked a peck on the cheek, or a little kiss on the lips every once in a while, and once Mel even patted me on the backside. We felt closer and more connected than we had in a very long time, and that night when we got home we made love, even though Mel had to get up at five A.M. to go to work.

"We're definitely going to do this again," Bonnie concluded.

THE TEN-SECOND KISS

For years I've asked the women in my classes whether they've ever felt lonely, desolate, and empty minutes after their mate has arrived home. The majority of women all nod in agreement. If you have this feeling too, I will give you a foolproof method to eliminate this particular problem. Tell your mate you'd like to try an experiment. For the next week every time you haven't seen each other for an extended period of time, you are to give each other a ten-second kiss. Tell him it doesn't matter how awful his or your day has been. You are to greet each other with a ten-second kiss. Time yourselves with a stopwatch initially so you can get accustomed to the length of this kiss. Most women hearing this for the first time don't think it's that long, but believe me, it's an incredibly long period of time. Try it by yourself so you can feel this kiss. What will happen after you initiate this assignment is that you'll feel very close and connected with your mate the entire evening. The first couple of minutes sets the tone for the rest of the evening. Most couples are used to greeting each other with a verbal response like, "Hi, I'm home," or "Anyone here?" There is no physical response, which is the reason that those isolated feelings are there. Once you begin this new way of relating to each other, feelings of closeness and warmth will replace those isolated feelings. You can then go about your normal activities such as preparing dinner, opening the mail, spending time with your children, or making necessary phone calls. The difference is that you'll feel connected to each other.

APPRECIATE THE MAN, NOT THE GIFT

Gifts are a wonderful way of communicating when words are uncomfortable or not enough. In the beginning of any relationship, cards and little tokens of your love are given and accepted graciously as a way of saying, "I'm thinking of you," or "I love you." In response we take care to acknowledge the other person's thoughtfulness.

As the years pass, however, we begin to make statements like, "You paid how much for this?"

"I can't believe you paid retail when I could have gotten it at a discount."

"That's much too expensive."

"I really didn't need that."

"I really don't care for the color."

"I don't look good in that," or

"What am I supposed to do with that?" I have always taught my children to think of the trouble the giver went through as they open each gift, rather than of the gift itself.

Especially after the holidays, the stores are filled with women returning gifts they received from their mates. Barbara, a woman in one of my classes who worked in the lingerie department of a large department store, told us that men spend so much time trying to find just the right nightgown for their wives or lovers that they practically drive everybody crazy. But when they leave, they leave feeling proud that they've found exactly the right thing. Then, the next day, the wife comes in laughing and saying something like, "Do you believe what my husband picked out?" Barbara said she often wished she could videotape the husbands as they shopped, because a woman who could see how much time and energy her husband spent making his decision would never return his gift.

I like to use the split-screen technique to teach women to be sensitive toward their mates. Mindy told the class that one day, while she and her boyfriend window-shopped, she noticed a wonderful pair of shoes in the window and commented that she'd love to have them.

On Mindy's birthday, her thoughtful boyfriend presented her with a huge carton, which Mindy proceeded to unwrap curiously. She couldn't conceal the disappointment in her eyes when she opened the box and saw the shoes she had admired in the window— six pairs of them, each pair in a different color!

Now, visualize a split screen and imagine what might have been going through her boyfriend's mind. He was probably thinking, Boy, I can't wait till she opens this box and sees the surprise. She's going to be thrilled to have the shoes she liked, and she'll have six different colors to choose from. Contrast his excitement and pleasure with the look of displeasure on her face.

I always want you to think about the intent when receiving a gift. If his intentions were to please you, don't communicate that you think his intent was wrong. Another student said her husband went to France and brought back a pair of seventy-five-dollar panties. When she learned how much they cost, she blew up!

"How could you spend that kind of money on an undergarment?" she cried. "You know how broke we are," she continued angrily, as she shoved the panties into a bureau drawer and vowed never to wear them.

Let's use the split screen again. What was he thinking? Probably, Since she couldn't come with me on this business trip, I want to bring back something really special for her. She deserves it. Contrast that with the woman's anger and her indifference to his sense of pride.

Somehow, as a girlfriend, we always appreciate our man no matter what gift he brings; but years later, as wives, we're concerned with how much it cost.

When I was on my honeymoon, I wanted my husband to select a fragrance that he really liked. He must have smelled ten different perfumes before he finally went crazy over one particular fragrance. He loved it! He said it was very sexy and alluring. I thought it made me smell like a French streetwalker, but because I was madly in love, I wore that expensive, "stinky" perfume until it was finally gone.

On our eighteenth wedding anniversary, my husband was so excited about the present he bought me that I couldn't wait to open it. You guessed it! There it was again, my stinky perfume! I had a split second to decide whether to tell him how much I've always hated that scent or whether to tell him how lucky I was to have a man who still remembers a special gift he bought for me on our honeymoon. I chose the latter, and we had a very romantic time that night.

My feeling is, What's the big deal if six days a week I wear a fragrance that I like and one day a week I wear what pleases him? Now I ask you, what's the big deal if once a week or once a month you wear a dress or an outfit that pleases your mate? What's the big deal if you have twenty paintings in your house and one of them is a gift from him that you're not particularly fond of? Hang it up anyway! What's the big deal if once in a while you wear the jewelry he gave you, even though you don't particularly like it? Someone liked it enough to design it. Someone liked it enough to stock it in their store. Your mate liked it enough to buy it. Wear it once in a while! You can wear the pieces you love the rest of the time.

Learn to appreciate the man, not the gift. Most men describe in great detail the trouble they went to purchase your gift. Appreciate his sacrifice, whether it was time or money. If you're lucky enough to have a man who sees something in a store and says, "Boy, my girlfriend (or wife) would look great in that," consider yourself lucky. Women who complain that their mates never give them anything usually find, upon reflection, that at one time they did buy them gifts, but were discouraged from continuing because of the women's obvious disappointment or negativity. Men whose mates are critical of their efforts will eventually resort to giving them the money to pick out what they like in order to avoid feeling foolish or buying the wrong thing.

Another graduate of mine told the class the following story as she showed us her eighteen-thousand-dollar diamond ring. Ten years before, when her happy husband presented her with this beautiful gift, my student immediately urged him to take the ring to a member of her family who was an appraiser to verify the value of the ring.

The appraiser felt her husband had been "taken"—by about three thousand dollars! To quote Sheila, "I lost more than three thousand dollars. It was the last gift my husband ever gave me."

A CRAZY-MAKER

Many women complain that their mates never have an opinion about where to go, what to eat, or what they should wear. I've observed that men start out in a relationship willing to make suggestions, but clam up when they are met with frequent objections. Most men want to please their women and make them happy. But when your husband suggests Chinese food for dinner after you have indicated that you don't have any particular preference and you say, "No, I'm not in the mood for that," you're being what is called a crazy-maker. You say one thing and mean another.

Perhaps you ask him to go shopping with you to

help you pick out a new dress. When he finds something he likes for you to try on, you say, "That's ugly. I could never wear that." Is it any wonder that he hates to go shopping with you?

Early in your relationship you ask him how you should wear your hair. He says, "I love it long." But do you care? No. When it becomes a nuisance, you go to the beauty parlor and have it cut short.

Once in a while, if you ask his opinion, respect it! Many men tell me that they no longer voice their opinion because what they think doesn't seem to matter. "She'll ask my advice and then do the complete opposite," they say. Just once in a while follow his suggestion and then tell him how much his opinion and advice mean to you.

My husband hates to go shopping but will always accompany me if I need help buying a dress for a special occasion. Do you know why? Because a few years ago, I bought a dress he thought I looked great in even though I didn't care for it. Ironically, I got more compliments on that dress than any other one I had ever worn. And every time someone told me how nice I looked or how much they liked the dress, I'd beam and say, "Thank you. My husband picked it out for me." My husband felt great every time I told him how many compliments I got, so the next time it wasn't very hard to persuade him to come with me to choose another.

ACTION ASSIGNMENT #3

Now take out another index card and write on it:

- **Listen, listen, listen—with my heart, not my head.**
  Let my mate know I understand what he is feeling, and reassure him that I am there for him. Don't criticize, evaluate, or give advice of any kind *unless* he asks for help.

- **Touch my mate every single day—starting to-day.**
  Pat his back, hug him, rub his back, hold his hand, kiss him, touch him on the arm or leg as we stand next to each other. Do anything that makes me connect physically with him. If I miss touching him on any day, I must make it up the next day by touching him twice as much.

- **Wear, use, or display a gift from my mate.**
  Take out a garment or piece of jewelry he may have given me, and wear it this week. Display or use a household item he gave me—and make sure he is aware of it.

- **The next time my mate makes a suggestion, follow it.**
  Follow my mate's advice and tell him how clever or smart he is. Compliment him for his wonderful ideas or problem-solving abilities.

5

ROMANCE IS A DECISION

I love getting feedback from former students who have put into practice what they learned in class. Deana was one of my best pupils, as the letter she sent me demonstrates:

I have been married for sixteen years and have a great marriage. But now, after taking your class, my husband, Bob, and I have reached a new stage of excitement in discovering each other all over again.

Bob is a very conservative, quiet, and reserved man. He is in the military and is gone a great deal of the time, and was away on a six-month assignment when I enrolled in your class. Recently he came home for two weeks of R and R (rest and relaxation), and I decided to try out a few of your suggestions.

I bought red light bulbs, black garter belt and stockings, Kama Sutra massage cream, and a lot of candles. I was extremely excited and nervous at what Bob's reaction might be. I was afraid he might laugh at me, or even think I was perverted.

Well, he did neither. He loved it, and we have discovered two new people in each other as a result of my risk taking.

I got the most wonderful letter from him after he returned to his assignment, which I wanted to share with you.

Regards,
Deana

Bob wrote:

Loving you, making love with you, has never been easier or more pleasurable than when I was home this last time. You revealed a new facet of yourself that was probably always there, but just kept under control.

I can't tell you how exciting you were. While many couples are hanging it up after sixteen years with each other, or out looking for affairs, you turn around and blossom into a woman comfortable and excited about her new (or newly revealed) sensuality.

Instead of looking back on memories, you've got me looking forward to possibilities. I can't ever remember finding you so lovely or exciting. You're going to have to be a little patient and wait for me to kick off my conservative cloak and inhibitions, as I try to match your newfound exuberance for loving.

It's scary—actually exhilarating—to have a wife, woman, lover with such a zest for life, herself, and the man she loves!

Those days together gave me wonderful memories and more important, a glimpse into the future with you. The kids are going to have to get used to closed and locked doors, nights away from them, and large smiles on my face, because I can't tell you how much I crave to be with you and love you.

Why am I so lucky to have a woman like you to love me? I wish I could express myself better. I'll keep trying until I get it right.

Love,
Bob

I'd say he expressed it very well!

This chapter is devoted to bringing out your femininity and enhancing the skills you need to change a relationship that has become boring and routine into one that is exciting and romantic. True romance is making a decision to let your mate know in many ways that he means more to you than anyone else in the world. It is saying, "I will do anything in my power to let you know that you are loved and that you really make a difference in my life."

It seems as if we know instinctively how to make our friends feel special, but when it comes to pleasing our mates we don't do as well. For example, if you were to go about setting a beautiful table and cleaning the house right now, would your mate assume you were having guests for dinner? Would he ask, "Who's coming over?" If so, it's time you made a similar effort just for him, so that occasionally you could surprise him and say, "No one, this is just for you!"

TIME OUT

The first question I ask a woman who is complaining about her relationship or her marriage is, "How long has it been since the two of you went away alone together—by yourselves—with no children and no friends?" Usually the answer is the same: "I can't remember," or "It's been at least three or four years."

There is no way a relationship can survive, let alone thrive, unless you take time out for just the two of you. That's why affairs are so wonderful. How long do you think an affair would last if you dragged along your parents, friends, or children with you wherever you went? Your marriage deserves the same kind of attention. You must make a decision that you will have a lifetime affair with your mate.

I believe that for a relationship to last, you must have what I call "date night" at least once a week. On "date night," you and your mate must spend the evening doing something alone together—just the two of you, no friends, no children, and no relatives. This evening must also be "childless," "timeless," and "jobless," meaning that your responsibilities and the pressures of your life should not be the focus of your attention. There are still six other nights of the week

that you can spend with friends, relatives, or problems.

That's the easy part. The next part is a little harder.
At least once every three months, you must go away
together for a weekend. An overnight stay at a hotel
qualifies as long as you get an early arrival and a late
checkout.

Now for the hardest part. At least once a year, you
must plan a vacation alone together for a minimum of
seven days. I know some of you are thinking, She
must be crazy. That's a great idea for someone who
has the time and the money, and no children, but
that's not my situation. I told you it was hard, but you
have to look at this "time out" as an investment in
your future. We're all familiar with the expression
"Someday you have to pay the piper." If you don't
use the time and the money now, for the good times,
I guarantee you'll be using it later to pay for the bad
times. If you don't spend the time and the money
now to provide a stable relationship for your family,
you're likely to spend a great deal of time and money
later overcoming your children's feelings of insecu-
rity.

For two-career couples, for whom money is likely
not an insurmountable problem, sacrificing family
time can cause guilt, especially if you already feel you
don't see your children enough. Just remember, the
happier and more relaxed you are as a couple, the
stronger your marriage is, the happier your children
will be. I go into guilt in much greater detail in Chapter Seven.

As I explained to my student Trudy over seven
years ago, the greatest gift you can give your children

is a loving, lasting relationship between you and your mate. The cost of taking a vacation is nothing compared to the cost of illness or divorce. We all know that the price of divorce is horrendous, both financially and emotionally. And believe me, if you don't take "time out," divorce or illness (or both) are likely to occur!

Recently, I got the following letter from Trudy, who wanted me to know what my advice had meant to her:

. . . when I came to you in tears, ready to end my marriage of fifteen years, you prescribed a one-week vacation for John and me.

After reciting all my reasons for finding such an idea impossible, you took the time to convince me that we owed it to ourselves and our children to spend whatever it costs to take that vacation on a yearly basis.

You even showed John, on paper, the cost of child care, food, lodging, and transportation for a one-week vacation, versus the cost of divorce. The difference was staggering! With the proof in black and white, there was no way we could deny the logic of your reasoning.

We took your advice, and even though many of our friends (some of whom are now divorced) thought we were crazy, we paid for the entire vacation with plastic. That time together somehow allowed us to become "man and woman" again, instead of "mommy and daddy," and our relationship benefited so much that we have continued to take a week's vacation together every year since then.

Thanks for your convictions, assurance, and knowledge.

You must find a way to build this kind of activity into your relationship, even if you think it's impossible. I've heard many creative solutions to the common obstacles to spending a week alone with your husband. For example, Barbara was a student in one of my classes who had three young children and worked full time just to make ends meet. Obviously, a week's vacation was a luxury she and her husband could not afford. Barbara solved the problem by making arrangements to trade one week of babysitting a year with a close friend.

When the time came for their "getaway," they would send the children to stay at her friend's house. Instead of getting in the car and driving away to a resort, or boarding a plane and flying somewhere, they returned to their own home, where they would make believe that they were in another place. One year, they made believe they were in a Swiss chalet, another in the south of France, and still another in Japan.

"We had so much fun making believe," said Barbara. "With the children gone, we felt like honeymooners. We looked forward to that week together for months.

"Breakfast in bed, making love in the afternoon, showering together, long walks in the evening, and just concentrating on each other in a way that wasn't possible with the children underfoot, renewed our love and fortified our marriage for another year.

"I don't know how we could have made it without these 'vacations,' " Barbara admitted.

"Even camping out can be a pleasure," Anita, another student, told the class.

"Going for a hike in the woods, holding hands, or sitting around the campfire at night is wonderful if you don't have to attend to anyone else's needs," she added. According to Anita, camping trips alone with her husband made them better parents, and they were always more patient and understanding with the children after they returned home from one of these trips.

LOVERS AT THE START, LOVERS TILL THE END

When you first fall in love, you and your man see each other only as lovers, and the time you spend together is intimate and very precious. Then, as the years go by and you become more and more entrenched in the role of wife, mother, professional, or parental caretaker, you may completely forget why you fell in love with each other. In the beginning, you appreciated, admired, and loved him exclusively. Inevitably, our lives become more complex and we are involved with many other people. There are children, friends, and aging parents, who demand much of our time and energy, and we begin to put less energy into our relationship and to take our mate for granted. Typically, what happens is that as the days become weeks, and the weeks become years, we suddenly realize that we are sitting across the dinner table from a stranger. You must not let that happen. To keep the romance in your relationship, you must be just his lover at least some of the time!

Most women find it extremely difficult to get fully into the role of lover in their own home. To most of us, home represents work. Even if there are no children present, it is still a workplace. There are beds to be made, marketing to be done, floors to be cleaned. Usually, expecting a woman to relax and let go in her own home is like expecting a man to relax enough to enjoy making love at work. Even women who are full-time career professionals don't see their homes as relaxing.

In order to feel completely relaxed, a woman needs to go to a hotel, a motel, or a resort. Trust me on this. I've talked to countless women who are surprised that they feel like completely different people whenever they get away from home for a vacation, but it's really no mystery. It's because they are separated, both physically and emotionally, from their homes and their workplace.

Most men, on the other hand, see their home as a refuge, probably because most men don't share equally in the work around the home on a daily basis.

In no way am I suggesting that you sacrifice your family vacations in favor of a vacation alone with your husband. On the contrary, you must take your family vacations *in addition to* your romantic vacations.

Before you start in with the usual, "How can she expect me to take two weeks off?" think about this. If you got the flu, you'd probably take off a week to ten days.

If you were in an accident, you'd take off a month or more to recover.

If there were a death in the family and you were emotionally distraught, you'd take time off.

Getting a divorce is so emotionally devastating that most women end up taking a leave of absence to regain their strength and a sense of balance.

Why must you wait for something negative to happen before you allow yourself time off? Take the time now for a wonderful, exciting, and romantic vacation. Please don't wait until it is too late.

CREATING A MEMORY

I often hear women complain that their lives (or their mates) are boring, but there is absolutely no excuse for anyone to be bored—ever! Since routine, predictability, and passivity are at the core of boredom, all you have to do to alleviate boredom is to change just one thing! For example, people are still talking about one of the most memorable dinner parties I've ever given. I'll never forget the look on our guests' faces as they sat down at the table and found, instead of knives and forks, rubber gloves at each place. "How strange," they must have thought. "Maybe she's planning to serve crab legs." Imagine their shock and surprise when the main course was served—and it was spaghetti and meatballs. We all laughed hysterically as we tried to eat the spaghetti, sauce, and meatballs wearing rubber gloves, without benefit of utensils.

That night I created a memory for everyone who was there.

Although there are many things in life over which we have no control, all of us are capable of creating memories. Remember, when we are old and gray, and all is said and done, we are left with only our memories. And what we remember best are those events that had special meaning—those crazy, out-of-character experiences—not whether we served mashed potatoes or baked, how the house looked, or what we wore. As someone once said, "You'll never remember the test you failed, but you'll always remember who you were with the night you decided not to study for that test." Start now to create the memories you and your family will cherish in the years to come.

Planning a surprise for your mate is one very direct way to show that you really care and to create a memory at the same time. The one receiving the surprise only gets to enjoy it while it lasts or as a memory, but you'll have the added pleasure of planning and executing the entire event. I always tell women to plan an "Oh, no, I couldn't. That's not me" kind of surprise, because when you do something that is completely out of character, your heart beats faster and your adrenaline flows. Do something unpredictable, spontaneous, and different. Don't worry that you're "not the type"—everyone has the ability to be creative and exciting. It just takes time, energy, and the willingness to try something different.

Pamela, in her words "a very conservative and straitlaced" lawyer in her thirties, is a perfect illustration of what can be done when you dare to be different. As she told my class, "I don't know what possessed me. I've never done anything like this before or since, but on the afternoon before my second wedding anniversary, I called my husband, who is also an attorney, at his office." "Hi," I said to him when he answered the phone. "I'm in room twelve of the X-rated Shangri-la Motel, lying on the bed completely nude, waiting for you."

Taken completely off guard, her husband asked, "Who is this?!" When Pamela replied, "It's your sexy wife and I'm waiting for my sexy husband," he turned to the client in his office and said, "It's an emergency. I have to leave right now. We'll have to reschedule our appointment."

Pamela told us he arrived at the motel within minutes and that he is still talking about their unforgettable second anniversary and the astonishing way in which she surprised him.

Another wonderful event was orchestrated by Gina, a vivacious blonde married to a very serious surgeon, who, as she says, "hardly ever cracks a smile." One Halloween night around 10:00 P.M., Gina told her husband she was going to the garage to finish the laundry and asked him to answer the door and hand out candy, should any more "trick or treaters" come by.

Grumpily, her husband muttered under his breath, "There'd better not be anyone out 'trick or treating' at this late hour."

When Gina reached the garage, she removed all of her clothes and donned a raincoat and an ape mask she had hidden there earlier. Quietly, she sneaked around to the front of the house and rang the doorbell. Her husband, still muttering, opened the door and found himself nose to nose with a nude woman in an ape mask shouting, "Trick or treat!" He was so startled he threw the entire contents of the bowl of candy he held into the air and stood frozen with surprise, unable to speak or move.

"To this day," Gina told us, "he begins laughing at the first sign of Halloween" because of the memory she created.

Whenever I feel bored, I ask myself what I could do that would be unpredictable and fun. One Valentine's Day, my husband was conducting a seminar at a nearby hotel, and I asked him what time the afternoon break would be, since I wanted to have a surprise delivered. Expecting flowers or candy (how boring), he told me they would break at about 3:00 P.M. Earlier in the week, I had purchased a large chocolate gorilla packed in a crate at a specialty store, and now I called a local company that specialized in singing telegrams and "special delivery" and had a man dressed as a gorilla deliver my gift to my husband at the seminar. I checked into a room in the same hotel and at precisely 3:00 P.M., as he was taking his break, the elevator doors opened and out stepped a 6'3" gorilla.

My husband told me later that when he looked up and saw the gorilla he prayed, "Please, God, don't let that be for me." Sure enough, the gorilla came looking for Mr. Kreidman and delivered the candy and my note, which said, "When you get through, come to room 555 so we can monkey around. I'm just ape over you." To this day, my "King Kong" remembers that Valentine's Day.

Another time, I was taking a very boring class, and to keep from falling asleep in class or dying of boredom, I tried to think of what I could do that would be fun and different. By midweek I had my act together. Before I left for my next class, I gave my husband an envelope that said, "Do not open until children are asleep. X-rated materials to follow." Inside was a note that read:

Darling,

The purpose of this note is to tell you how much I love you and how important you are to me. I will be thinking of you all through my "boring class" and how I can't wait to come home to your arms.

Now, for further instructions go to your third drawer and open the box you'll find there.

Love from the most important person in your life.

Your Wife

In his drawer, he found a box on which was written, "X-rated materials enclosed." Inside the box was a list of instructions and various items. The instructions were as follows:

1. To provide a romantic atmosphere, replace those boring white lights in our bedroom with the enclosed red bulbs.

2. Spray your favorite perfume on pillows to provide a heavenly scent (my "stinky" perfume was enclosed).

3. Run a hot bath with lots of bubbles for sexy wife (bubble-bath crystals were enclosed).

4. Shave and prepare yourself for lots of love (shav-

ing cream and razor wrapped in ribbon were enclosed).

5. Have everything ready by 9:00 P.M. so that if class gets out early you'll still have plenty of time.

6. Remember—*you* are the most important person in my life and I LOVE YOU!

That night was not only exciting for my husband, it was also very exciting for me. For once I wasn't bored in class. As I thought about my husband preparing himself for my homecoming and anticipating what would happen when I got there, I felt as excited as a bride. And from the moment I started planning that surprise the week before, I was in a good mood. By the way, my husband still keeps the notes I wrote to him that night among his important papers.

HIS NEEDS, YOUR NEEDS

One of the most important differences I've found between men and women is that while men need to know you find them sexually attractive in order to give you the emotional fulfillment you crave, women must feel emotionally fulfilled before they can react to their mates' physical needs. So there you have it—the ultimate impasse. He requires something completely different to react to your needs than you require to react to his. Or to put it another way, "A man gives love for sex. A woman gives sex for love." So what is the solution to this dilemma? The answer lies in your ability to understand that, although his way of loving is different than yours, he loves you nonetheless.

I find that many men have a difficult time articulating their feelings. It is easier for them to express their love sexually than verbally. When I polled a group of men, the majority, when asked "What is the most pleasurable time you spend with the woman you love?" responded, "When we are making love." Women, on the other hand, say they are happiest when they are hugging, touching, kissing, or engaged in a meaningful conversation with their mate.

A man needs to feel loved, not endured. Many women perform the sex act as if they were paying their dues or fulfilling an obligation. In *The Hite Report on Male Sexuality,* hundreds of men were asked "Why do you like intercourse?" The psychological or emotional reason men gave most often for liking and wanting intercourse was the feeling of being loved and accepted that intercourse gave them. One man summed it up by saying, "Intercourse continually reaffirms my close attachment with my mate. It tells me she loves me. It gives me confidence. It makes me feel wanted."

In my classes, I hear men talk about their sexual feelings more openly than most women are privileged to hear. Harold, for example, even after being married for eighteen years, still feels like a schoolboy if he and his wife have planned an overnight getaway at a motel.

"I get so excited thinking about it that I'm putty in her hands for the entire day before, just to be sure she'll be in a good mood for lovemaking," he confided.

Bob, another student, told us that he and his ex-wife got along fine outside the bedroom, but every time he wanted to make love he felt like he was imposing. "Whenever I approached her, she'd give me a look that said, 'Oh, no. Not again.' It made me feel so awful that I finally stopped asking."

Eventually, Bob found a woman who welcomed his loving and who restored his self-esteem. "She initiates sex a lot of the time," Bob said, "so I don't feel rejected, like I did with my ex-wife."

Jonathan, a very shy man, had never thought of himself as much of a lover. "Betsy was the first girl I ever went to bed with, so I have no one to compare her to," he bravely told the class one night.

"All I know is that I never want anyone else," he continued.

"She's always telling me how much she wants me, and what a great lover I am. I know what I've got, and I'll never trade her in for another woman!"

EMOTIONAL LOVE VERSUS
PHYSICAL CLOSENESS

I know many women wonder how there can be sex without love, but my question to you is, how can there be love without sex? Remember this important principle: In order for a man to give to you emotionally, he has to have his physical needs fulfilled—he needs to know that you desire him sexually. For most men, sex is the most important confirmation of your love and his self-worth. It is only when he feels fulfilled that he will consider your emotional needs.

PROVOKING THE SENSES

To those of you for whom creating a romantic atmosphere is a new experience, I recommend starting with baby steps. It isn't necessary to go to extremes in order to set the stage for a romantic encounter. After being bombarded all day long with sunlight, bright lights, and fluorescent lights, a good first step to creating a romantic atmosphere is to stock up on red light bulbs. The flattering light provided by these inexpensive but indispensable objects will make you look like a sex goddess—slim and wrinkle-free (this could be the reason certain areas are called "red light" districts). You can find them in most hardware stores, and if you happen to be embarrassed, wait until Halloween to buy them. Imagine your mate's surprise when he turns on the table lamp and sees a soft red glow instead of the usual bright white light. If he asks, "What's this?" you can reply, "I love you, and since red is the color of love, I wanted to fill the room with love."

LIGHT THE WAY TO ROMANCE

Candlelight is another easy and effective way to create a romantic setting. It's no accident that fine restaurants use candlelight to create an intimate setting. Most people immediately begin to feel calm and relaxed when they walk into a dimly lit room.

Listen to how one of my students used candles to surprise her husband, a salesman who was frequently away on business trips. One time, when he arrived home from a trip, he found a note on the front door addressed to him. It said, "Welcome home. I've missed you."

When he stepped into the entry hall, he saw a trail of candles leading all the way up the stairs, one candle on each stair. Joan had taken small paper bags and rolled down the edges, filled them with beach sand, and put a long, tapered candle into each one. When her husband reached the bedroom, he found the bed entirely surrounded by candles, and on his pillow was a single rose and a note inviting him to join Joan in a bubble bath.

Speechless, he went into the bathroom and saw Joan soaking in the tub by the light of two candles, one on either side of the tub. At a loss for words, all he could say when he saw her was, "Wow—you look great and I feel great!" Now, follow Joan's lead and on your shopping list write: Buy red light bulbs, tapered candles, and lunch bags. Get beach sand and matches and have fun.

SET THE STAGE FOR LOVE

Music is another good way to stimulate the senses and create a special mood. We are continuously assaulted by loud noises, telephones, sirens, planes, typewriters, screaming children, and people shouting. As if that weren't enough to numb the senses, don't forget TV, which (according to the Nielsen report) is on approximately seven hours a day in the average American household. *Shut it all off!* Instead, turn on some soft, sexy music. Everyone's taste in music is different, but you can experiment until you find what's best for you. Music can also be the starting point for a very special kind of evening.

For example, Sharon surprised her boyfriend one night with a "theme dinner." That day at work he received a huge box that contained a kimono, a pair of slippers, and a note from Sharon that said, "I'm having a wonderful dinner tonight, and I'm hoping that wonderful you will attend. Enclosed is everything you need to wear in order to be appropriately dressed." Her boyfriend told Sharon later that he could barely concentrate on work that day as he anticipated the evening ahead. That night, when he arrived at Sharon's apartment, the first thing he noticed was the sound of the wonderfully soothing Asian music that created an instant feeling of adventure. Sharon knew how important it was to eliminate the distractions of daily life, and she created an atmosphere of romance with imagination and music. You can create a "theme night" too. Here are some suggestions:

- Hawaiian Hiatus—complete with luau for two, robe, slippers, several leis for his neck, and Don Ho singing the Hawaiian Wedding Song.
- A Night in Spain—Flamenco music, a mantilla for your hair, and a highly suggestive note in Spanish accompanied by a Spanish–English dictionary so he can translate it.
- Moroccan Feast—Moroccan music, a veil for you and a burnoose for him, and no utensils. Feeding each other salad, chicken, and vegetables using only your hands can be very sensuous.

- Venice Vacation—Red-checkered tablecloth, candles in wine bottles, Pavarotti, and pasta will make a Latin lover out of any man.
- Greek Picnic—Lamb on a skewer, togas, and music from *Zorba the Greek* lead up to a dessert of baklava (you can lick the honey off his fingers when he's through).
- Japanese Tea Party—Be shy and seductive in a kimono and sandals as you observe the ancient ritual of the Japanese tea ceremony. Don't forget to hide your smile behind a fan, letting your eyes talk for you.
- African Safari—Create a jungle setting, give him a bush jacket and pith helmet, and call him your "big, brave hunter."
- Li'l Abner and Daisy Mae—Make this a summertime picnic with fried chicken and potato salad. Furnish your backyard with a bale of hay, wear Daisy Mae shorts and a tight blouse. Give him overalls (but no underwear). Let dessert be a roll in the hay.
- Ski Weekend—Skintight ski pants, hot buttered rum, and a soak in a steaming hot tub should put you both in the mood for making love on the bearskin rug in front of the fire.

BE HIS FANTASY

Another way to create a romantic feeling is with visual stimulation. Keeping in mind that most men are very stimulated by what they see, buy yourself something that is visually appealing and different from what you normally wear. Ask your mate to go shopping with you for a garment that he would enjoy seeing you in. You can have a wonderful day together looking for a negligee that turns him on, and even the most frugal man will usually spend lavishly if he's asked to purchase what pleases him.

Another visual turn-on for most men is the wet T-shirt contest. Why not create your own at home, just for him. Buy several T-shirts, put them on wet, and see which one he likes best.

NO EXCUSES, PLEASE

Are you beginning to get the picture? You must go out of your way to give him the message that you went to all this trouble for him—not for the neighbors, not for your friends, not for the children—just him, because he is the most important person in your life. Keep in mind as you plan your day or evening together that you are creating a memory that will last forever. The variety of things you can do to create a romantic memory are endless, once you begin to think about it. I know it seems like it's just too much to do. Women who work outside the home tell me they just don't have enough time, and women who are full-time mothers usually use the children as an excuse. Well, I'm not saying you have to do this all the time. How about every three months? Isn't your relationship worth going that extra mile for just four times a year? The sexual problems that send some couples to a sex therapist are almost always the *symptom* of a relationship that has gone stale, rather than a sexual problem per se. Making the effort to create a memory can go a long way toward preventing such problems.

I love to tell a particularly moving story about a woman named Dee who complained that every night her husband came home from work and insisted on having dinner served upstairs in his bedroom while he watched TV.

When I asked Dee if her husband had ever come home to find a candlelight dinner and his wife waiting in a seductive outfit, she laughed derisively. "Are you kidding? I have four children under the age of twelve and a full-time job!"

My reply to her was, "How would you like to have four children under the age of twelve, a full-time job, and NO HUSBAND? Because that's what you'll have if things continue in this way."

With some difficulty, I persuaded Dee to approach some of her neighbors and ask if they would watch her children for one night, if she would do the same for them. They all jumped at the chance, and Dee proceeded to plan a special night for herself and her husband, Ned, without telling him about it.

When he came home on that special night, he almost passed out from shock. Was he in the right house? Who was that gorgeous woman? What was that wonderful aroma? Where was that beautiful music coming from? He was absolutely stunned by the magical evening Dee had planned. They made beautiful love all night long, and Ned, whom Dee had never seen cry, wept in her arms as he told her how much he had missed her being his lover.

Take time to stop and smell the roses. Take time to do something unpredictable. Take time to do something out of the ordinary. Take a baby step toward a giant change in your boring life!

SAY IT WITH BALLOONS

Another great way to send a powerful message is with balloons. This is what Denise did. One evening while her boyfriend slept, she had an extra set of keys to his car made. The next day, while he was at work, Denise drove into his company's huge parking lot and parked near his car. Then, working right out of her car, she proceeded to use an air tank (you don't use helium because the balloons will fly away!) to blow up dozens of balloons, each of which she had already stuffed with different messages telling her boyfriend why he was so special.

As she worked, a crowd gathered, intrigued with what she was doing. A few of the onlookers even began helping her, one man tying knots in the balloons while another woman helped Denise stuff the balloons into the car. By the time she was done, the entire car was filled with balloons.

As a last touch, Denise taped a very large needle to a note and placed it on the windshield. The note said, "The only way you're going to be able to get into this car is to pop each balloon and read the message inside that tells you why you are the most incredible man I have ever known."

One of the onlookers commented, "I hope your boyfriend knows he's the luckiest man alive, having a girlfriend like you!" Envy was evident on everyone's face.

Her boyfriend was so touched by Denise's grand gesture that that evening he came calling with flowers and candy—and tears in his eyes. Denise created an event that will live forever in her boyfriend's memory. Do you think he'll ever let this woman go? Would he want to spend the rest of his life without this woman who went to such great lengths to let him know he is loved? Denise too has joined the ranks of women who have created a memory forever.

TEACH ME TONIGHT

Some of you are probably wondering why the responsibility for romance falls on your shoulders. "Why is it always the woman?" you ask. The answer is because most men have never learned how to be romantic: They need to be taught. Men are accustomed to operating out of the logical side of the brain. It's the women who buy the romantic novels and read the love stories. When I read a romantic novel, all my husband is interested in are "the good parts," and when it comes to movies, he'd much rather see an action-packed film like *Rambo* than something mushy like *Love Story*. Women's magazines have endless advice on how to be romantic, sexy, and appealing; but, tell me, when was the last time you saw an article in a men's magazine on how to be a more romantic lover? Chances are, your man didn't learn anything about romance from his parents, either. So, if he doesn't read about it, see it on the screen, or grow up in an atmosphere where romance is prevalent, how is he going to learn unless you teach him?

When asked, men who are romantic attribute their knowledge to a woman who has played a part in their lives. Some were lucky enough to learn about romance from mothers who actually taught them what women respond to and how they like to be treated. Others have learned from their sisters. Still other men have had women leave them because they weren't romantic enough, so the second time around they are trying to do things differently.

ROMANCE IS AN ACQUIRED SKILL

Romance is an acquired skill that has to be taught. Although falling in love might just happen, having a loving relationship does not. Having a loving relationship requires nurturing; and it requires skill and knowledge. You can either lead by "telling" or you can lead by "showing." In my opinion, leading by example is the most powerful way there is to teach another human being what it feels like to be romanced. Don't wait for him to instigate romance. You take the lead and show him how wonderful and exciting it is to be showered with affection and attention. Later, you can ask him in a nonthreatening way to try his hand at returning the favor.

Keep in mind that he must feel completely safe before he will try something that feels foreign to him. You can gently coax him into using his underdeveloped creativity by setting an example rather than by making demands. Chances are, if he feels safe, he will respond to your request to plan a surprise for you and be willing to take that baby step—to try something that he has never done before—and chances are he'll find that it feels good.

KING FOR A DAY

This is what a student of mine named Wendy did to introduce her boyfriend to the fine art of romance. She bought a crown and placed it on his bed with a note saying, "This crown signifies that you are my king, and on Saturday you will be crowned 'King for a Day' and the entire day will be devoted to your pleasure."

Saturday began with Wendy serving him breakfast in bed, followed by a massage, and then a sensual shower for two. She had prepared a picnic basket in advance, and they picnicked in a secluded place in a nearby park. While her boyfriend napped, Wendy quietly left and was picked up by her girlfriend at a predesignated spot.

When her boyfriend awoke, he found a note instructing him to get ready for an enchanted evening. "In order to do this," the note said, "go to Jack's video store, where there is a package waiting for you."

Off he went to pick up the first in a series of packages and notes that Wendy had arranged for earlier. At Jack's he was given an X-rated movie, wrapped with a ribbon, and a note saying, "Although you've just been handed an X-rated movie, it is nothing compared to the X-rated evening you and I are going to have. Now go to Sheila's Lace Shop for further instructions."

At Sheila's another package awaited him, as well as

a note that said, "I know how much you like black, so in this beautifully wrapped box is something that is soft, silky, clingy, skimpy, and black."

The next stop was a liquor store where several bottles of wine were waiting for him with another note saying, "We'll have our own wine-tasting party tonight."

The last stop was a fragrance shop, where he was given a package consisting of half a dozen perfume samples and another note, which said, "Tonight we will have a private fragrance test. I'll apply these perfumes to strategic spots on my body and it will be your job to match the perfume on my body to the correct bottle."

By this time, Wendy's boyfriend could hardly contain himself. When he arrived home, the apartment was softly glowing with candles and red lights, and romantic music was floating through the rooms. On the bed was a pair of bikini underpants and one last note saying, "Please wear these. I want to see as much of your gorgeous body as possible."

What a wonderful day this lucky man had had. In his arms later that evening, Wendy asked if she could be "Queen for a Day" sometime. And of course his reply, as he kissed her, was "yes."

Wendy was smart. Instead of having a long intellectual conversation about how her boyfriend wasn't meeting her needs, she set an example. You need to show your man how to make you happy, and you need to let him know how good it feels to be the center of attention.

For those whose imagination may be a little rusty from lack of use, I have provided a list of fifty-one foolproof ways to keep his fire lit. As you read the list, you will automatically focus on the activities with which you feel most comfortable. SKIP THEM!

I want you to choose the ones with which you are uncomfortable. I want you to stretch—to go beyond your normal limits. Surprise your mate. No. SHOCK HIM!! Knock his socks off—and don't forget to have fun.

FIFTY-ONE WAYS TO KEEP
HIS FIRE LIT

1) Send him on a "love hunt."
This is like an old-fashioned treasure hunt, where further instructions are waiting at each destination. If you are very clever, you can make the instructions cryptic, so that it takes some imagination to decipher the clues.

Have a note delivered to your mate explaining the rules, and telling him to follow the instructions precisely and he will be rewarded! Send him from place to place to pick up a purchase that has been made in advance and that is waiting for him with additional instructions. The following are some of the places you can send him:

- Liquor store—where a bottle of good champagne is waiting with his name on it.
- Florist—where a bouquet of flowers is waiting.
- Party supply store—for a dozen balloons that say "I love you."

- Record store—for his favorite tape.
- Your favorite restaurant—where he finds you waiting for him.

After dinner, excuse yourself and tell him you're going to the ladies' room. As you leave, discreetly slip him a note that says, "After this lovely dinner, I thought it would be nice to have dessert at the (fill in the blank) hotel. Wait at least ten minutes before you leave. I'll be waiting for you in room (fill in the blank)."

2) Plan a surprise half-year birthday party.
Invite all of his friends to celebrate his thirty-fifth and one-half, fifty-fifth and one-half, or whatever, birthday. This would be a much greater surprise than a party on his birthday.

3) Have a photo session with your mate.
Tell him he's better-looking than most male models, and that you want some good pictures of him for your desk or wallet, so everyone can see how handsome he is. Pose him in a business suit with a briefcase; in jeans, a cowboy hat, and boots; pajamas; scanty underwear; and if you have a Polaroid, pose him in the buff.

4) Give him a manicure.
Make everything ready ahead of time—clear polish, clippers, soapy water, lotion for his hands.

Tell him how strong and powerful his hands are, and how they need special care. Massage his hands before starting the manicure.

5) **Entertain him in the bathroom.**

Arrange a profusion of candles in the bathroom. Prepare a bubble bath. Pour two glasses of champagne to toast away the cares of the day. Get into the tub and then call to your mate, "Honey, I forgot a towel. Could you please bring me one?" (I'll bet it won't take him more than ten seconds to join you in the tub.)

6) **Take him to a drive-in movie.**

Relive your teenage years and steam up the windows.

7) **Forget your underwear.**

Just before you enter the restaurant or your friend's house, tell him you forgot to put on your panties.

8) **Tie him up.**

Use silk scarves to tie his hands and feet (loosely) to the bedposts. If your bed isn't properly equipped, use a chair instead. Tease him a long time before finally making love to him.

9) **Say it with stick-ups.**

Use those little sticky pads to leave notes for him in unexpected places, so that he'll find them as he gets ready for work in the morning.

Put the first one on the inside of the toilet seat, so that when he flips it up he sees a note that says, "Take care of my favorite part of your body." Put a note on the bathroom mirror, so he'll see it when he shaves, telling him how much you love his face. Leave him messages on the toaster, the milk carton, in his briefcase, on the dashboard of the car—all of them telling him how wonderful you think he is.

10) **Fill the bed with rose petals.**
Tell your mate that life with him is a bed of roses, as you make love to him in a bed of roses.

11) **Advertise.**
Put an ad in the personal column of your local paper, letting the whole world know how much you love him and how wonderful he is. List a few of his most outstanding qualities in the ad.

12) **Take a ride in a limousine.**
Rent the movie *No Way Out* and watch it together. The following week, rent a limousine and reenact the scene in the movie that takes place in a limo.

13) **Take him out to the ball game.**
Surprise him with tickets to his favorite sports event —and go with him!

14) **Kidnap him.**
First make the necessary arrangements at his place of employment. Then, walk in unannounced and hold a toy gun on him while you place toy handcuffs on his wrists. Take him away for an "afternoon delight."

15) **Do it with style.**
Be his own personal hairstylist. Wearing a very short barber's smock with a garter belt and stockings under it, greet him as if he were a new customer. Brush up against him suggestively as you shampoo his hair and

blow it dry. Tell him things like, "I've fantasized about running my fingers through your hair from the moment I first saw you."

16) Use your hands.
Prepare an elaborate dinner and serve it with no silverware. Tell him you have to feed each other with your hands.

Be prepared to experience anything—from a return to the joy of your wedding day when you fed each other a slice of cake . . . to hilarious laughter . . . to sensual finger-licking.

17) Give him a ring.
Call him at work to tell him you love him. Then tell him what you're going to do to him that night when he gets home from work. Be outrageous!

18) Play ball.
If he played football in school, make love to him on the football field. If he played soccer, make love to him on the soccer field, and if he played basketball, make love to him in the gym. If he was a spectator, make love to him under the bleachers!

19) Give him a present.
Yourself—all dressed up in nothing but stick-on bows.

20) Take the train.
Take a train ride in a private car and leave the driving to them.

21) **Plan an overnight getaway.**
Arrange for a baby-sitter, then meet your mate at the door with a packed bag and tell him the two of you are "running away from home."

22) **Go western.**
Leave a cowboy hat on the front seat of his car or send one to him at work. Attach a note telling him to meet you at a certain motel that night. End it with, "You'll be back in the saddle tonight, cowboy."

23) **Have a slumber party.**
Fix a sleeping bag for two on the floor in front of the fireplace, with a bottle of wine and a bowl of popcorn. Tell each other secrets, such as your favorite fantasies.

24) **Have an *aromatic* evening.**
Discover the romance of scent. Collect a supply of perfume samples. Dab a bit of each perfume in different spots of your body, and then have your mate match them up with the samples.

25) **Take a walk in the rain.**
Wear your raincoat and galoshes—and nothing else. When it's safe to do so, show your mate that you're nude under the coat.

26) **Pull the plug on the TV.**
Send your nightgown, sprayed with his favorite perfume, to your mate at work. Attach a note that says, "Tonight I'm turning the TV off and turning you on!"

27) **Immortalize him.**
Make a scrapbook for your mate entitled This is Your Life. Dedicate it to a "very special man." Start with a baby picture, and tell his life story with photos, special awards, clippings from news articles, pictures of his trophies, photographs from school in his football uniform, honors received from work—anything of special importance. Leave it on the coffee table for all your guests to see.

28) **Ring his bell.**
Call your mate at work and hint at a special evening. Tell him to hurry home—you'll be waiting with bells on. Greet him at the door wearing bells on your wrists and ankles—and nothing else!

29) **Give him a balloon bouquet.**
Fill his car with balloons that have notes in them telling him the many ways you love him. Tape a needle to a note and put it on the windshield, telling him he has to pop all the balloons and read all the notes before he can get into his car.

30) **Send a "no occasion" gift to him at the office.**
Surprise him with flowers, candy, balloons—even jewelry.

31) **Be subtle.**
Make a large banner that says SANDY LOVES AL and hang it on the garage door, or somewhere along his regular route to work.

32) **Take him for a ride in a hot-air balloon.**

33) Write "I love you" across the sky.
Hire a skywriter to write your message in the sky. Plan a walk on the beach or in an open field at the appointed time. Tell him you wanted the whole world to know how special he is.

34) Say it with music.
On his birthday, arrange for the local high school band to march down your street playing "Seventy-six Trombones," and "Happy Birthday to You."

35) Take him to the "red light" district.
Replace the white bulbs in your bedroom with red ones to create a romantic atmosphere.

36) Challenge him to a game of cards.
Strip poker, that is.

37) Give him breakfast in bed.
Invest in a beautiful tray. Set it with a sparkling white linen place mat, china, crystal, and silver. Place a rose on the tray, with a note promising love in the afternoon.

38) Take a walk in the moonlight.
Make a wish upon a star together.

39) Play Santa Claus.
Around Christmastime, dress up as Santa Claus in a sexy red and white negligee. Ask him if he's been naughty or nice, and tell him Santa has something special for "naughty boys."

Encourage him to tell you what forbidden things he wants for Christmas.

40) Go trick-or-treating.
At Halloween, dress up in a mask and a coat. Wear nothing underneath. Ring your front doorbell when he doesn't expect it, say, "Trick or Treat," and flash him.

41) Be the Easter bunny.
On Easter, wear bunny ears and pink pajamas with feet. Fill an Easter basket with goodies, including massage cream, body paints, champagne, and, of course, some chocolate. Just be sure you buy it at a specialty store that sells erotic chocolates.

42) Go stargazing.
The next time there's to be a meteor shower, plan to spend the night on a blanket in the desert. Find a secluded spot, break out the champagne, and lie back and watch the stars. Let nature take its course.

43) Play Jane to his Tarzan.
Rent some tropical plants, and decorate your bedroom like a jungle. Give him a loincloth, and you wear a leopard-skin bikini. Serve a bowl of nuts, fruit, and berries. Feed him grapes, one at a time, while jungle drums play in the background.

44) Be the maid for a day.
Some Saturday when you have housecleaning on the schedule, send the children to a baby-sitter. Rent a maid's costume with a very short skirt and wear it

with a black garter belt and stockings, and very high heels.

Tell your husband you've hired a French maid for the day, and begin to clean the house in a very seductive way. With a French accent, ask him, "What is your pleasure, sir?"

45) **Be a blonde (or a redhead).**

Send your husband a sexy note and sign it, "From your secret admirer." Arrange to meet him at a nearby bar or restaurant at an appointed time and day. Tell him to look for the blonde wearing a red rose on her lapel.

If you're a brunette, get a blond wig and dress differently than you normally would. If you're a conservative businesswoman who usually wears suits, wear a short black leather skirt.

If you're already a blonde, get a red wig. The idea is to get completely out of character. If you usually wear miniskirts, then dress conservatively. Wear a business suit (without a blouse), and a pair of horn-rimmed glasses.

Just remember, your goal is to shock him and make him feel as though he is with a completely new woman.

46) **Take to the woods.**

Rent a secluded cabin in the woods, with no TV, no

telephone, and no radio. Talk to each other and get reacquainted.

47) "X" marks the spot.
Make reservations at an X-rated motel. Give yourself permission to be wicked.

48) Treat him like a king.
Make him "King for a Day." Cater to his every whim and surprise him with special treats.

49) Give him a massage.
Buy a book on how to give a massage. Use a nice massage cream, and spend at least an hour massaging him. Leave the best for last.

50) Be a character.
Plan a theatrical evening for two. Go to a costume shop and rent period costumes for both of you. You could be Scarlett O'Hara and he could be Rhett Butler, or you could be Josephine and he could be Napoleon.

Whatever you choose, stay in character, and spend the evening seducing him as that character.

51) Stay afloat.
Charter a sailboat for the night. Have a gourmet dinner catered and sip and sup on the high seas.

A fantastic complement to any of the above ideas is a new romantic board game by Decifer Inc., which is based on the principles I teach. It's called *How to Host a Romantic Evening*. The game enables you to have an evening of fun, romance, and intimacy. It's a wonderful way for you to create a memory. If you have a problem finding it in your local game store, send a self-addressed stamped envelope for more information to L. H. F. Enterprises, P. O. Box 1511, El Toro, California 92630.

There you have it—fifty-one ways to keep his fire lit. This entire list has been compiled from suggestions made by women who have experienced the joy, the pleasure, and the power of being a woman. Use your power as a woman to make your man the envy of all friends and coworkers.

ACTION ASSIGNMENT #4

On another index card, write:

- On a regular basis, find creative ways to show my mate how much I want to have a love affair with him.

6
NEVER POSTPONE HAPPINESS

Women who come to the Light His Fire workshop are sometimes surprised to learn that being a good mate goes far beyond paying your man compliments and wearing a sexy nightgown. It also means taking responsibility for your own happiness, a challenge that many of the women in my classes have accepted —some with hesitation and fear, others with excitement and joy. To my knowledge, none of the women who accepted the challenge have been sorry.

Recently, I spoke with a former student named Janice, who had taken my class more than six years ago. She told me she had first become aware that she didn't know who she really was or what made her happy after she started Light His Fire.

Janice said, "I'm embarrassed to admit it, but I was

one of those women you describe who only thought of herself as somebody's daughter, somebody's mother, and somebody's wife. I defined myself by other people."

Janice went on to tell me that since taking my class she had returned to college and had earned her degree and her teaching credentials. She currently teaches home economics at the high school level.

She told me proudly how supportive her husband and family had been as she was studying for her degree, and about the gift her husband, Martin, gave her when she graduated.

"The trophy he gave me is among my most treasured possessions," Janice said.

She went on to read the inscription, which said, "To my wife, who was always an important, intelligent woman—only now she knows it!"

Some of you may feel that your mate is responsible for your happiness. Well, he isn't! Each one of us is responsible for our own happiness, and anyone who sits around and waits for someone else to make her happy is going to be very disappointed and unfulfilled. As any mother knows, being with small children twenty-four hours a day is physically exhausting and mentally numbing. When my children were very small, I, like many mothers, expected my mental stimulation to come from my husband. Each day I'd anxiously wait for him to return from work, anticipating that he would share his day with me. Unfortunately, the man who came through the door at the end of the day was even more miserable and frustrated than I was. He was physically exhausted and mentally drained, and had very little to give. What resulted was a stalemate. He expected me to make him happy, and I expected him to entertain me. So much for expectations!

I didn't realize it at the time, but by continually postponing happiness for some future time—by saying, "When my husband comes home, then I'll be happy"—I belonged to the "if only" club. If any of the following statements sounds familiar to you, you may be a member too:

If only I lost ten pounds, I would be happy.

If only I had more money, I would be happy.

If only I had a baby, I would be happy.

If only I had a bigger house, I would be happy.

If only I were prettier, I would be happy.

If only I had more <u>fill in your own dream</u> (talent, intelligence, ability), I'd be happy.

If you are a member of the "if only" club, you're robbing yourself of the only thing any of us really have—the present! When we live in the past or focus too much on the future, we rob ourselves of the now!

BE HERE NOW

Some of you who are reading this book have already experienced changes in your relationship. As you received new information, you acted. You read suggestions for change and improvement and you implemented them.

On the other hand, some of you have postponed doing the assignments for one reason or another. Perhaps you have told yourself you're too busy at the moment, or you're too tired, too confused, too unhealthy, too fat. You say you'll try these ideas next week, next month, next year!

Next week, next month, or next year may never come.

The time to start having a love affair with your mate is now. The time to buy that beautiful dress is now. The time to make an "I love you" call is now. The time to take control of your life and happiness is now.

Don't be like Arlene, a student of mine in her late twenties. Instead of concentrating on the present and making every day with her lover count, Arlene always worried about the future and constantly asked her boyfriend when he was going to marry her. I didn't need a crystal ball to know that Arlene would have no future with this man if she continued to nag him about it.

I advised her to focus on the present, making each weekend they spent together as intimate and fulfilling as possible, so that he would look forward to being with her the following weekend. Eventually, her boyfriend would not want to live without her, and by concentrating on the now, Arlene would be assuring her future with him and, more important, making their now far better. The truth is, no one has a crystal ball, and life doesn't come with a guarantee.

As I finished telling this story in class one evening, a woman named Melinda slowly stood up and, with tears in her eyes, told the class to pay attention. "I wish I had known this before," she said.

"Last weekend I got the shock of my life. My husband, with absolutely no warning, announced he was moving in with his secretary, packed his bags, left."

Melinda was devastated. She had really believed that her marriage would last forever. "I just kept telling myself that after the children were grown, we'd be able to spend more time together. I put our relationship on hold, and boy am I sorry!" she concluded sadly.

I can think of countless examples of women who have postponed happiness and regretted it. There was Heidi, who stayed in a job she disliked, hoping to be promoted into a better position. After she'd stuck it out for two years, on the promise of being promoted, Heidi's company declared bankruptcy and Heidi was out of a job.

Busy Norma kept waiting to call her grandmother until she had enough uninterrupted time to make it a long call. She knew they had a lot to talk about, and she wanted to be sure they wouldn't be hurried. When Norma's grandmother died suddenly, it was too late. It had never occurred to Norma that her strong, iron-willed grandmother wouldn't be around forever.

Don't make the same mistake these women made. Begin now—not tomorrow, not next week, but today —to seize the moment and make this day count! Remember, yesterday is gone and tomorrow may never come. Today is all we have.

Kathryn joined the class hoping to make a decision regarding marriage. She had been in love with Jay for nearly three years and couldn't imagine life without him, but she was hesitant to commit to marriage. Because her parents had divorced when Kathryn was fourteen, and because many of her friends were also divorced, Kathryn was afraid her marriage might end in divorce too. "What if we get married, and it doesn't work out?" she worried.

"What if you get married, you're very happy, and one of you gets killed in an accident?" I countered.

"What if you get married, you're happy, and a major earthquake causes California to fall into the Pacific Ocean?" I continued facetiously.

Kathryn got the point. She was in love now, and had been for the last three years. There was no point in playing "what if." She realized we have no control over what happens in the future. There are no guarantees. There is only the present.

Too many women postpone happiness for one reason or another. I know pregnant women who can't wait until their babies are born. Don't miss out on the wonder of the miracle growing inside of you in anticipation of a future event; enjoy every moment of your pregnancy. I know women who can't wait for their children to grow up. Enjoy your children now and at each stage of their lives. Time passes much too quickly as it is—don't hurry it along. Women with grown children are quick to tell you that the years have flown by and the kids have grown up in the blink of an eye! I know women who avoid marriage because they're afraid they won't stay in love forever. Don't postpone your life together because of what might happen ten years from now!

SAVOR THE MOMENT

I read a book to my class by Shel Silverstein entitled *The Missing Piece*. Even though it's a children's book, it has a universal message. It is the story of a circle that has a part missing. It searches and searches for its missing piece, just as most of us are always looking for that "piece" of fulfillment we think is necessary for our happiness. When the circle finally finds its missing piece, it realizes that the search was more meaningful and exciting than the final result. As the circle learned, what really counts in life is each moment of our journey—not our final destination.

John Lennon said, "Life is what's happening to you while you're making other plans."

Whenever I feel myself drifting back to the past or dreaming about the future, I actually say to myself, "Ellen, be here *now*!" That means when I'm in the beauty parlor having my hair washed, I concentrate on the experience—the wonderful feeling of having someone massaging my scalp—instead of worrying about the phone calls I have to make when I leave.

Life is made up of millions of moments, and once a moment is over, it never comes back again. We have to enjoy the moments as they happen.

This point has been made particularly clear by some of the older members of my classes. Mabel, a woman in her seventies, told the class that she had spent most of her life worrying about things that never happened. She said she spent the entire time her husband was in the service worrying that he might be hurt or killed.

"Every time the phone would ring, I was paralyzed with fear," Mabel said. "I was sure it was bad news.

"I was afraid to leave the house, because I might miss a phone call saying he was injured and he needed me," she went on.

As it turned out, her husband returned from the war unharmed, and Mabel went on to worrying about other things. Looking back, she said she realized that all of her worrying was wasted energy that could have been spent on productive activity. She wishes now that she had used the time her husband was overseas to go to school and learn something useful. "Somehow I guess I believed that by worrying I could affect the outcome. Now I know better," she said.

Lucille, a seventy-two-year-old student, confessed that she had spent most of her life worrying about problems that existed only in her mind. She had played "what if" games repeatedly. Games such as:

"What if we have a nuclear war?"

"What if the children drop out of school?"

"What if my husband becomes ill and can't take care of us?"

None of these events ever came to pass, Lucille said. "Our lives were really quite worry-free," she laughed. Her advice to the class was to take inventory of what you have today, and let tomorrow take care of itself.

Most of what we worry about is trivial. It is important to keep things in perspective. A good rule of thumb is to analyze what it is you are worried about. Is it something that will still matter ten years from now? If not, then it isn't worth worrying about now. What you serve next week at a dinner party, the fender-bender you just had, or the fact that you spent twenty-five dollars more on a dress than you had budgeted are all unimportant in the big picture, and are not worthy of worry lines. If it won't matter ten years from now, let it go! Just make up your mind that you're not going to worry—and then don't.

Although it is important to understand your past, to learn from it, and to grow from that knowledge, it is also important to let it go, for it no longer exists. While it's wonderful to have dreams, hopes, and goals for the future, it is even more important to live each moment of your life *now,* because that is all there is.

NEVER PUT OFF TILL TOMORROW

Let me tell you a true story about an eye-opening experience my husband and I had on a cruise to Tahiti. We had stopped at Bora Bora for lunch at one of the most beautiful hotels in the world. We started talking with an elderly couple at a nearby table and learned that they had taken off three months to tour this part of the world. We would be returning home in another few days, and I was green with envy and said so.

The woman turned to me and said, "Don't envy me. It is I who envy you your youth and health. Last year I almost died. I have cancer, and although I was able to plan this trip, I'm in a great deal of pain. At your age, when we were healthy and could have enjoyed it, we couldn't afford a trip like this. Now that money is no object, I'm having a tough time just getting out of bed each morning."

Her husband turned to mine and said, "You know, the time between when you can finally afford your dream vacation and the time when you die is so short that you should actually take that trip when you can enjoy it—whether you can afford it or not."

We both nodded in agreement and felt we had received an important message.

When we returned to the ship, I saw my fellow passengers in a new light. Many of them were in their seventies and eighties. Some were in wheelchairs, some were even blind, and I thought to myself, What a crazy world. Here we are in a place that is breathtakingly beautiful and full of places to explore, and some of these people can't fully enjoy it. Why do people wait until they are old to take a trip like this?

That experience, combined with the following story told by one of my students, has convinced me that the time to take your dream trip is now.

Ann, a retired high school teacher, related that she and her husband, Harold, had planned for years to see the United States in a motor home when they retired. Money was no object, and they had their eye on the most spacious and luxurious model available.

Just a few weeks short of his retirement date, Harold had a stroke and has been confined to a wheelchair since. Sadly, Ann and Harold's dream vacation will always be just that—a dream.

Don't wait. Go now. Borrow the money, if necessary, and pay it back when you're eighty. And if you can't pay it back then, so what? That may sound frivolous, but I'm dead serious.

Don't postpone—doing, buying, experiencing—until you have the time, the money, or the perfect opportunity! That time may never come!

OUR THOUGHTS CREATE OUR MOOD

If you are frequently depressed and there is nothing physically wrong with you, you probably need to change how you think. Whether you realize it or not, your thoughts and your beliefs are largely responsible for how you feel and what happens in your life. The belief that there is nothing you can do about your life or your situation, in particular, will lead to depression. Most of the time helplessness is nothing more than a state of mind, which you have the power to change. Instead of wasting energy on negative thoughts, you need to spend your energy solving the problem. You need to take action. Instead of focusing on feeling out of control, say to yourself, "I don't particularly like the situation I'm in and, although I'm not sure at this point what to do, I will come up with alternatives so that I am once again in control."

YOU'RE IN CHARGE

Usually, just taking some kind of action will put you back in control and end your depression.

If you feel helpless because someone has hurt you, insulted you, criticized you unfairly, imposed upon you, given you something for less value than you think is fair, or is in any way responsible for the pain or discomfort you feel, you must confront them.

It does you no good to complain to those who have no control over the situation. If you don't like the ice cream that is served at the ice-cream parlor, don't complain to the kids who serve the stuff—it's not their responsibility. Go to the person who can correct the situation—the owner or manager! The key to getting satisfaction is in complaining to the right person.

Letting the person in charge know you are unhappy accomplishes two things. First, it places the responsibility for dissatisfaction where it belongs and where it can be dealt with in a way that will satisfy you. And second, you feel good about yourself because you have taken charge of your own happiness. You are not acting as a victim; you are in control.

Don't use fear as an excuse to avoid taking responsibility. If fear is keeping you from acting, just feel the fear and do it anyway!

FACE UP TO FEAR

When we don't deal directly with the people who hurt us, we tend to dump our feelings on the people we love. For example, it's not unusual to suppress the anger we might feel at a stranger, and then direct that same feeling at our partner, later. You know the syndrome—you had to wait in line at the bank because there weren't enough tellers; it took forever to get three items at the supermarket because only one checker was open; you went to pick up the dry cleaning and it wasn't ready, and instead of complaining to the manager you just grumbled to the person who waited on you.

When you get home, you finally let out all of your frustration—on your undeserving mate or children—screaming, "You don't know what it's like to deal with these uncaring idiots at the bank (supermarket, cleaners)! You have no idea what I put up with all day long."

Late in my first pregnancy, my husband and I were living in an apartment with no washer and dryer.

One Saturday, my husband dropped me off at a nearby laundromat to do the wash, and said he'd be back to get me in an hour. After he drove away, I realized I had left my money at home, so I went next door to the liquor store and explained the situation to the owner. When I asked him if I could borrow a dime or use his phone to call my husband, he looked at me and said, "Get out of my store. I don't give money to people off the street, and no—you can't use my phone." Completely humiliated, I walked the eight blocks home, crying all the way. After that, whenever I passed that liquor store, my stomach would knot up, my heart would pound, and I would feel ill. I knew that the only way I could get rid of this pain was to confront the man who had caused it, and I decided I had to go back to the liquor store after my baby was born even though the thought of it scared me.

I waited about three months, and then one day I got all dressed up, took a friend with me for moral support, and went back to have my say. I approached the counter where the same man was standing and said, "Excuse me. Three months ago I came in here and really needed to borrow a dime or use the phone and you wouldn't let me. Now, I'd like to leave you this dollar so that you can be kind to the next ten people who may need to borrow a dime."

The man grabbed the dollar out of my hand and threw it at me, snarling at me to get out of his store. I was glad to leave, but when I got to the door I turned and said to him, "I'm going, but before I do, I want you to know that you are a cruel, insensitive man, and I feel very sorry for you and the people who have to be near you."

The miraculous part of this story is that once I had told the store owner how I felt, I was able to pass the liquor store and not feel ill. The episode that had taken place more than three months before was finally complete.

Even if you don't have a similar situation to contend with, you probably have a mother-in-law, a friend, a neighbor, a relative, even a mate—someone with whom you have an unresolved problem—whom you need to confront.

Many women don't confront their mates because they're afraid of driving them away. These women don't want to "make waves." They believe peace and harmony are insurance against the threat of being abandoned by their mates. Interviews with men reveal quite the opposite, however. They say there is nothing worse than being on a date with a woman who has no opinions, for example, or with one who agrees with everything a man says. In addition, men whose mates leave all the decision making to them feel burdened.

A woman who values herself and her needs will gain the respect of her man. Connie, for example, had tolerated her husband's sarcasm for years rather than cause a scene. Finally, after one particularly humiliating experience that took place with friends, Connie decided she wasn't going to take it anymore.

The following weekend her chance to make a stand came while Connie and her husband, Dan, were out with a business colleague of Dan's and his wife. When the wife started to give Connie directions to her house, Dan blurted out sarcastically, "Are you kidding? Connie gets lost going around the block. She'll never find your place."

Normally, Connie would have laughed Dan's comment off and covered up her anger. This time, though, she was determined to have her say. As difficult as it was for her, Connie swallowed hard, took a deep breath, and then confronted her husband.

"Why did you say that, Dan?" she asked. "You know I have a great sense of direction."

Shocked, her husband backed down immediately. He apologized, saying, "Hey, I was only joking. I didn't really mean it."

Later, when they were alone, Connie told Dan how much his sarcastic remarks hurt her. She told him she wasn't going to tolerate them anymore. "The next time you put me down in front of someone, I'm going to get up and walk out," she said.

Connie's strength came through, and Dan realized she meant it. "I won't do it again," he promised.

Carla, like many of the women in my classes, was a people-pleaser. Because she wanted everyone to like her, she found it very difficult to assert herself.

Carla's in-laws lived in Minnesota, and for many years they had been in the habit of paying an extended visit to Carla and her husband during the month of January. After listening to the class discussion about fear, Carla decided she needed to assert herself with her husband first, and then with her in-laws, telling them that this year, instead of playing hostess, she wanted a vacation.

"As I thought about it, I realized that in my desire to be liked, I had gone overboard in being a good hostess. It was no wonder Sid's parents liked to visit. I catered to their every need, waited on them hand and foot, prepared gourmet meals every night, and spent my days acting like a tour guide.''

Carla rehearsed everything she would say to her husband in her mind as she reassured herself with the knowledge that the worst that could happen was that he or her in-laws would say no.

Sid was responsive to Carla's suggestion that maybe, just this once, his parents could baby-sit for the children while Sid and Carla took a trip. He offered to call and ask his parents, but Carla insisted that she wanted to do it herself. She knew she had to "feel the fear and do it anyway."

The in-laws were actually delighted to baby-sit. They had been yearning for an opportunity to spend time alone with the children, but hadn't wanted to impose.

"It all worked out beautifully," Carla said. "The children got to know their grandparents better, my husband and I renewed our relationship, and I got over my feelings of resentment."

As you will learn in the next chapter, unexpressed feelings never go away. If you don't give them a voice, they will eventually be expressed as illness or disease. Even though the idea of confrontation scares you, you need to feel the fear and do it anyway, so that you can complete your unfinished business. If you wait to do something that is difficult for you until you aren't afraid, you'll never do it. Nobody is fearless. Even the most assertive women I know tell me that they are often afraid to do or say something that is particularly hard for them. Many of them take classes in assertive-ness training, hoping to overcome their fears.

Janet, a very attractive woman in her forties, revealed how fearful she felt the first time she attended a "singles" dance. Divorced for six years, Janet had not dared to venture beyond her daily routine of job, home, children, and close circle of friends during that time. Finally, she decided she was tired of being alone.

Janet related that she was so frightened as she entered the dance hall that she thought she might faint. "I couldn't breathe," she remembers. "My palms were clammy, I could hear my heart pounding in my ears, and I was so tense I could feel myself jerk with each step I took."

Janet says she doesn't even remember being asked to dance, but suddenly she realized she was in a man's arms as he waltzed her around the floor. Gradually, she began to relax a little.

Each time she went out after that, it became a little easier. Janet says she's glad she began to go out again, in spite of her fear. "If I had waited until I wasn't afraid, I'd still be sitting at home, instead of planning my wedding," she said, beaming.

Even seasoned performers will tell you they are afraid each time they have to go onstage, adding that it gives them the extra energy they need to give an outstanding performance. The first time I had to do a seminar for an audience of five hundred, I was scared to death. That moment when I had to step onto the stage was as terrifying to me as having a loaded gun held to my head would have been. But I felt the fear and did it anyway.

Sometimes talking to yourself will help alleviate your fear. Many of the risk-takers I know ask themselves, "What's the worst that can happen?" They draw a "worst-case scenario" to give themselves the push they need to go ahead with a scary task. Then they feel the fear and do it anyway!

TO THINE OWN SELF BE TRUE

Respect yourself. Commit yourself to the belief that you are the most important person in the world. If you don't have self-respect, chances are no one else will respect you either. Self-respect comes from being true to yourself, from feeling good about who you are: It comes from letting other people know how you truly feel. So, be true to yourself, confront the people that hurt you, and complete your unfinished business.

Some years ago I asked a group of men to list some of the traits they found desirable in a woman. I was somewhat surprised when their answers focused on personality traits, rather than physical characteristics. Over and over, I was told that women who are happy and who feel good about themselves are the most attractive.

"If a woman isn't happy, then she's no fun to be with," wrote one man.

"I like a woman with confidence in herself," wrote another. "It doesn't matter what she does, as long as she feels good about herself. There are too many women and too little time to be with someone who feels unfulfilled or angry," he went on.

Many men confessed that they had been driven from a relationship with a woman because of the woman's basic unhappiness. "I finally left, because I realized I couldn't make her happy," lamented one man.

Another said, "My wife expected me to be her social director, her constant companion. She never left my side. I just couldn't go on living with a woman who was always longing for more than I could give."

Obviously, men think women who are happy and fulfilled are a turn-on.

LISTS, LISTS, LISTS

I make it a practice never to go to bed at night without making a list of what I need to do the following day, with the things I want to do least getting top priority. It doesn't matter what it is—making a phone call, going to the cleaners, returning an unwanted purchase, or talking to a potential client—once I write it down I don't have to worry about it anymore.

They say the stewing is worse than the doing—that it takes three times as much energy to worry about what needs to be done than to actually do it. Just imagine! It takes three times more energy to worry about making that dreaded phone call than just to pick up the phone; three times more energy to worry about cleaning the house than to get out the mop and get busy.

Did you ever go to bed completely exhausted and wonder why you were so tired when you hadn't done anything all day? Chances are you did something—

chances are you spent the day worrying. Worry is a waste of energy and accomplishes nothing. Being active energizes you—worry drains you.

Remember, if what you're worried about isn't something you'll remember ten years from now, it's probably not worth worrying about at all. What you serve for dinner is not something you'll remember in ten years, so just go buy something and cook it. The stewing is worse than the doing.

Don't waste your energy on worrying—you'll have no energy left when it comes time to act. Procrastination takes energy. If you put off doing the things you don't want to do, you won't have the energy left to do the things you do want to do.

TIME FOR YOURSELF

Be sure to include taking care of yourself on your daily list of things to do. Do you know why? Because you are a very important person and because you are worth it! Imagine yourself as a large pitcher filled to the brim with a red liquid. The red liquid is love. Now, picture some empty glasses that represent your mate, your children, a relative, a friend, a neighbor— anybody who needs your love or requires something of you. For example:

CHILD: "Hey, Mom. Can you do me a big favor? I need to write a report. Could you buy some typing paper and a nice cover?"
MATE: "Honey, we have to go to a company banquet, so keep next Sunday open."

MOTHER: "Sweetheart, this is your mother. Would you mind going shopping with me? Dad and I are going on vacation and I don't know what to buy."

BOSS: "Mary, I need these reports on my desk by five o'clock tomorrow."

NEIGHBOR: "Hi. Could you do me a favor and watch Billy? I have a doctor's appointment."

FRIEND: "I'm so depressed. I really need to come over and talk to you."

As you respond to each of these requests, imagine that some of your love liquid is being poured into each cup. What happens to the pitcher (you) as you fill up everyone else's love cup? It (you) becomes empty. And when you're empty, you have nothing left to give.

By being good to yourself—by including yourself on your list of things to do—you refill your "love cup" (the pitcher). Being good to yourself means different things to different people. For some it might mean a manicure; for others it could be a massage. It might mean a trip to the beauty shop, reading a good book, taking a bubble bath, taking a trip, buying a new dress, attending a seminar, gardening, or taking a nap. It doesn't matter what you do, as long as it's selfish.

Each day that you give of yourself and empty your pitcher, you have to be selfish in order to get that pitcher full again. Every time you fill up, you have more to give. Love is like knowledge. The more you have, the more you can share. You can only give what you possess. If you don't love yourself and care for your own needs and wants, you'll have nothing to give to the people you love.

On the advice of a friend, Rita, a woman who had given up a rewarding career to become a full-time mother, had enrolled in my class. Rita knew she felt angry and resentful, but until she saw the "love cup" demonstration in class, she wasn't sure why. After class she approached me to say that she now realized she was bone-dry. "With a two-year-old and a four-year-old, I never have a moment to myself," she sighed.

I asked her what would fill up her love cup.

"I'd love to have a baby-sitter for a few hours each week," she smiled wistfully, "so I could just soak in the tub and read a good novel."

At my urging, Rita discussed the idea with her husband, and with his approval she made the necessary arrangements. Her attitude improved immediately, and so did her relationship with her husband and children. Rita had learned the importance of being filled up in order to give to the people she loved.

You can use the "love cup" to explain to your children why you are going shopping alone or why you and Daddy are taking a trip. Actually fill a pitcher with colored water and use it to fill empty glasses as you explain to them that, "Mommy will have her love cup full to give you more love." Show this to your mate and tell him, "I'm going to this seminar so that I can feel good about myself, and when I do, I can love you more."

By the way, don't expect people to read your mind. They don't know whether your love cup is full or empty. Only you know that. If you insist on giving to others when you're empty, you'll either have a physical breakdown or a mental breakdown. And worst of all, you'll hate yourself. You can't give what you don't have! Don't be a martyr. You have to tell the people around you what you need.

If you think, My husband should know what I need. My neighbor ought to know how tired I am. My kids should be aware of the stress I'm under. You're not being fair. Tell them!

If you're too tired to prepare the dinner you had planned, tell your mate, "Honey, I'm really exhausted. Let's order takeout food or go out to eat. I'm not up to making dinner." Going out to dinner might be just what you need to fill up your love cup and let you feel much more energetic and loving. Don't be afraid to be good to yourself. You deserve it!

YOUR CUP RUNNETH OVER

During the past eight years, I have collected ideas from women in my classes about ways that they fill their love cups. Maybe some of these ideas will help you take better care of yourself.

- Hire a housekeeper to come in every week, or every other week.
- Hire a baby-sitter for a few hours each day or each week.
- Schedule a long luncheon with a friend.
- Go on a shopping spree.
- Experience a one-hour massage.
- Have a professional pedicure.

- Have a professional manicure.
- Have a professional facial.
- Attend a fashion show.
- Become active in a cause you feel is worthwhile.
- Join a gym and stick to a workout schedule.
- Take an aerobics class.
- Get a new hairstyle.
- Have your colors analyzed.
- Take a long bubble bath.
- Spend one hour a day reading a good book.
- Take music lessons.
- Take dancing lessons.
- Take acting lessons.
- Take a day off and spend it in bed, eating chocolate bonbons and watching TV.
- Go back to school.
- Spend a day at the beach alone.
- Plan a ladies' night out. Splurge and rent a limo.
- Take a gourmet cooking class.
- Join a dining-out club.

WHO AM I?

In order to be happy, we have to know ourselves—to know what it is that we really enjoy doing. I believe we all begin life knowing who we are and what makes us happy, but we leave our true selves behind in an effort to please the meaningful adults in our lives. As children, we are bombarded with "shoulds" until we eventually buy into other people's ideas of what we *should* be and what we *should* do.

What you *should* be and what you *should* do is

whatever you feel most comfortable being and doing. You must be true to yourself. Don't try to conform to other people's expectations of you. The most important person to please is yourself. If you are happy, everyone who is touched by your life will benefit.

We often hear stories about people who pulled themselves up by their bootstraps and who achieved their goals against all odds. But I know that for every one of those who achieved their goals there are at least a thousand others who didn't pursue their dreams because they weren't encouraged to do so. As children, we assume that because our parents are older and wiser and because they love us, what they say must be true. If they told us:

You have an awful voice,

You will never be an artist,

You're too shy to act,

You're too clumsy to be a waitress,

You're too short to be a model,

You don't have enough brains to go to college, we believed them. You can't change the past. Your parents and the other influential people in your life said what they believed to be true. That doesn't mean it was true. As an adult, you can decide on a different belief. You can now decide to believe in yourself.

FOLLOW YOUR HEART

We all have an inner guide that tells us what is true for us. We just need to have enough confidence in ourselves to follow our guide. I can't emphasize strongly enough how important it is that you listen to your guide.

Please take the time to sit quietly with your eyes closed, and ask your guide, "Who am I? What do I want to do?" I promise you'll get an answer if you really try.

One of my students had a difficult time getting an answer from her inner guide. She came to me terribly upset and said, "I don't know who I am. I know I'm Peter's wife, Kira's mother, and Fred and Gertrude's daughter. But I don't know who ME is!"

I told her to try again, but this time she was to make believe her husband didn't exist, her children didn't exist, her parents didn't exist, money was no object, age was not a factor, and time was no problem. Sometimes we have to overcome what we perceive to be obstacles before we can hear what our inner guide has to tell us.

The second time my student tried the exercise she was more successful. She came back to me saying that secretly she had always wanted to be a doctor, but she felt that at age thirty-two it was too late.

"Of course it's not," I told her. "If you take one baby step every day, at the end of the year you will have completed three hundred sixty-five baby steps, which equal one giant step. The first step might be to call the local college and ask them to send you a catalog. Another baby step might be to set up an appointment with a counselor. Then just take one course to see if you can pass. Then another and another, and eventually you'll be ready to apply to medical school." I told her it might take ten years, but even becoming a doctor at forty-two would give her many years of practicing medicine. After all, in the words of one of my students who received her college degree at age seventy-three, "I figured I was going to be seventy-three anyway, so why not be seventy-three with a degree rather than seventy-three without one?" My student would be forty-two anyway. She might as well be forty-two and a doctor.

I had the privilege of having two wonderful women in my seminar who were attorneys. Both had been legal secretaries for many years, and both had secretly dreamed of becoming lawyers. They started law school, where they met, when they were in their early forties. By taking baby steps and taking just one class at a time, they were able to achieve their dream and are now partners in their own law firm.

After completing my class, another graduate, who had always wanted to be an actress, decided to enroll in acting classes when she was sixty years old. She called to tell me she looked forward all week to her acting class and how thrilled and fulfilled she felt.

Does she have to be discovered by Hollywood? NO! She has discovered herself, her own unique talents.

TWO QUESTIONS FOR SELF-DISCOVERY

Shakespeare said, "This above all: to thine own self be true, and it must follow as the night the day, thou canst not then be false to any man." To be true to yourself is to be in a state of grace. To find out if you are being true to yourself, ask yourself these two important questions:

1) If I weren't getting paid for what I'm doing, would I continue to do it?

If the answer is yes, you're doing what you want to do. The truth is, I would teach this class for free, and sometimes have, because I believe in it and love what I'm doing.

2) If I only had one year to live, would I continue to do what I'm doing?

If the answer is no, then why don't you stop? You could die within the next year, and you would have wasted your last year doing something you didn't want to do.

One evening after class a new student came up and asked if she could talk to me for a few minutes. She confided that she was on the verge of divorcing her husband. She told me he was impossible to please.

"He's always made fun of me for being what he calls an 'artsy-craftsy' person, so recently I enrolled in a class to learn how to become a travel agent. Now, he complains about all the homework I have to do, and what a low-paying profession I've picked."

I asked Paula what she wanted to do. She said she wanted to please her husband.

"Nothing you do will please your husband," I told her. "Why not think about pleasing yourself?"

I asked her the two important questions. If she only had a year to live, would she want to be a travel agent? If she couldn't get paid to do it, would she want to be a travel agent?

Paula looked shocked and said of course not. If she only had a year to live, she would want to spend it painting and making handcrafts.

I invited Paula to accompany me to a highly successful arts and crafts center in our area, and asked her if she might like to own something like this some-day. She rolled her eyes and said if she could own a shop like that, she would think she had died and gone to heaven.

The last I heard, Paula was taking classes at the local community college on how to start and run your own business.

Since I started Light His Fire, I have heard so many women say, "I gave up everything for that man. I did everything I could to please him, and he left me." Of course the men left! When you give up everything, you give up yourself. Nobody wants to be with a sponge or a parasite, or even worse, a "nothing." When you give up you, you cease to exist.

I remember two men in particular who ended up leaving women who contributed little or nothing to the relationship. One of them, John, told me that he eventually left his wife, Kelly, just so she could have the opportunity to discover who she was.

In John's words, "She had become a total bore. If I asked her to tell me about her day, she would just say that nothing interesting had happened."

If he asked her what movie she would like to see, or where she would like to go for dinner, she always answered that she didn't care. Finally, John couldn't stand it anymore. He told Kelly he was going to stay with a friend.

"The truth is," he said, "I'm really enjoying it. It's so much fun being with someone who has an opin-ion, and who has some experiences to share."

Another man told me his wife wanted his approval

for everything. Initially, he liked it, he said, but eventually it began to drive him crazy.

"She's gotten to the point where she even asks my permission to go to the supermarket."

When he tells her, sincerely, that he doesn't care, she takes it to mean he doesn't love her.

"Come to think of it," he said, "maybe I don't love her anymore. It's too much responsibility to be the one who makes all the decisions."

These women gave up everything to make their man happy, hoping he would never leave them. Instead, they created the very thing they were trying to prevent. If, on the other hand, these women had remained true to themselves, they would have continued to change and grow, and that turns a man on. Such change and growth may be hard for him to accept in the beginning, but in the long run it will gain his respect, one of the key ingredients in a lasting relationship. Remember, conflict leads to growth, and either you grow or you die.

ACTION ASSIGNMENT #5

On an index card, write:

This card is just for me.

- **Be here now!**
  Stay focused on the present.

- **Let go of worry.**
  If what you're worried about won't concern you ten years from now, let it go.

- **Make plans now for a fabulous vacation.**
  Don't wait until it's too late to take your dream trip.

- **Feel the fear and do it anyway.**
  Complete unfinished business. Don't be afraid to rock the boat.

- **Keep my love cup filled.**
  If you fill your love cup first, you'll have more to give to the people you love.

- **Get organized.**
  Write a list of things you need and want to accomplish every day. Remember, the stewing is worse than the doing.

- **Believe in myself.**
  Be led by your inner guide, not by other people's expectations.

7

FEELINGS JUST ARE

One of the most common reasons that husbands and wives fail to communicate is because they actually fail to recognize their own feelings.

For example, Linda, a student in one of my recent seminars, told me that it wasn't until after the session on feelings that she was able to understand why she had felt so alienated from her husband and unable to respond to him for the past few weeks.

Linda recalled that two weeks before my class, they had entertained her husband's best friend and his wife for dinner. Linda was still nursing their three-month-old son, and right after dinner she excused herself to feed the baby.

As she left the table, Linda overheard her husband's friend make a smart remark about the baby getting more attention than the father. To her annoyance, Linda's husband answered in kind, instead of defending their joint decision to have the baby breast-fed. Although she hadn't felt it was significant at the time, Linda later came to realize that she was deeply hurt by her husband's insensitivity.

After the class on feelings, Linda found an opportunity to explain to her husband how this incident had affected her. He held her in his arms and apologized, and later wrote her this note:

> Dearest,
> I'm sorry I hurt you. I didn't realize what I said would make you feel so bad. I just wasn't thinking.
> Since the baby came I have been feeling kind of left out. I've really been missing our old closeness.
> I'll try to be more understanding. Please forgive me.
>
> I love you.

You are the only one who knows how you feel, and your feelings can change from one moment to the next.

During one twenty-four-hour period, you could experience disappointment, love, confusion, anger, joy, sadness, and resentment. Even more amazing is that you may have exactly the same experience as another woman, yet your feelings about the experience will be completely different.

For example, one married woman may be elated to learn that she is pregnant, while another woman of the same age and marital status may be devastated by such news.

Three women who arrive late to a class may have three different reactions. One woman may feel relieved that she has finally arrived, the second may be annoyed because the instructor started without her, and the third may be concerned that she has missed something important.

Which women had the "right" feelings in response to their situation? All of them. Our feelings are neither right nor wrong. They just are. No one has the right to tell us how we should feel. We do, however, have the obligation to support our own feelings and not pretend that they are unimportant.

To be true to yourself, you must understand that feelings can never be labeled right or wrong. Feelings just are. They belong to you and must be *recognized, shared,* and *aired.*

Couples who are willing to share their feelings are much more likely to experience good communication and real intimacy than couples who hide their feelings. Sometimes, however, it may take several attempts before communication actually begins to take place. The first few times you tell your mate how you feel, you may be told that you're silly to feel the way you do, or that you shouldn't feel that way. Your obligation is to stand behind your feelings. You can respond by saying, "It may be ridiculous, but that's the way I feel." Don't be afraid to rock the boat. Your mate may become angry or withdrawn for a few days, but eventually he'll come around.

The trick to standing your ground without inciting a riot is to use "I" statements instead of "you" statements. For example, Marla, armed with new knowledge about how to get her needs met, returned home after class to confront her boyfriend, Sam, about his flirting.

She told him how jealous she was when he flirted with other women, and when she gave him a specific example, Sam became angry and not only denied that he had been flirting, but told Marla she had no right to feel that way.

Marla responded by saying, "I want to feel special when I'm with you. I want to feel like I am the only woman you have eyes for. I don't like to feel like I'm competing with another woman."

Sam left in a huff, and Marla didn't hear from him for several days. She was beginning to worry that she shouldn't have rocked the boat when Sam finally called. He apologized for his behavior and told Marla that he wouldn't flirt in the future. When Sam confessed that Marla's jealousy made him feel important, Marla realized that he really cared for her, and that she needed to let him know he was important to her in some way other than by displaying jealousy. By sharing her feelings honestly, Marla had gained new knowledge about Sam's feelings for her, a promise of changed behavior, and a new-found intimacy with Sam.

DON'T ATTACK, ASSERT

Both Linda and Marla got favorable responses to their assertiveness, because they approached their mates in a nonthreatening way. They accepted responsibility for their feelings, saying, "I feel . . ." rather than "You made me feel . . ."

If you tell your mate he made you feel a certain way, it will be perceived as an attack and he will automatically defend himself. The result will be an argument, instead of understanding and intimacy. If, on the other hand, you stick to saying how you feel, your mate will be more receptive to your message.

Repeat the following statements, listening as if they were being said to you, and notice the difference in how you feel as you hear them:

"Why can't you remember to call when you're going to be late?"

"I worry when you're late and I haven't heard from you."

Can you hear the difference? Remember, it's important to make "I" statements and to stand by your feelings.

WE TEACH LYING

I believe we all start out in life being in touch with our feelings and are able to share them in a completely truthful and honest way. For example, a child around two or three years old, if asked "Did you break that toy?" will proudly nod his head up and down to signify yes. The child has been completely honest, but most parents will punish him anyway. Typically, they will say, "You're a naughty boy. Go to your room," or "Now I have to punish you," teaching the child that if he tells the truth he will be punished. Parents will also say something like, "You really hurt me," or "You really upset me." So children also learn that if they tell the truth, they hurt Mommy and

Daddy. Normal children who lie are only lying for one of two reasons—to protect themselves or to protect their parents.

Children are even taught how to lie in the classroom. When a teacher asks, "All right, who was talking?" the one who owns up to it, the one who takes responsibility for what he did, is sent to the principal. The reaction is never "Thank you for telling the truth and taking responsibility, John. Please try not to distract the class. If you are bored, I'll try to give you something more stimulating to do." The pat on the back, the compliment, is enough to quiet the child.

Is it any wonder that as adults we are still lying? We're just acting on what we learned as children: telling the truth equals punishment for me or pain for my loved one.

Betsy and her husband had recognized this pitfall early in their marriage and had made a pact that they would always tell each other the truth, and that no matter how much the truth hurt, they would respond by saying, "Thank you for being honest. I love you."

According to Betsy, it wasn't always easy, but after forty-three years of marriage they still kept the pact.

"I never had a problem with my husband calling to tell me he was going to be late, because he knew he wouldn't get a lecture," Betsy told me.

"There were times, though, when I really had to bite my tongue," she added.

If your man lies to you, it's either because he doesn't want to cause you pain or he doesn't want to get into trouble. It's up to you to make it safe for him to tell the truth. You might start from scratch, saying, "From now on there will only be praise, hugs, and kisses for telling the truth." As difficult as it may be, assure him that the pain of not knowing something is greater than the pain of knowing. Now watch out! You will be tested! Don't fail!

BOYS DON'T CRY

Many women think that their husbands have no feelings—or that somehow men don't have the same kinds of feelings that women do. But the truth is, there is no difference between how little boys feel and how little girls feel—the only difference is in the way our society treats them.

The following story is a perfect example of how a boy gets the message that it's not okay to cry. My son's Little League coach had an adorable four-year-old son who was the team "bat boy." It was his job to run and get the bats. One time he got in the line of fire and a baseball hit him right in the stomach. As he stood there holding his tummy and crying, his father yelled at him, "Bat boys don't cry! Do you hear me? Bat boys don't cry!" I felt like hitting the coach over the head and then asking him, "Do coaches cry when they're hurt?"

Another time, when my son was six years old, he fell off his bicycle and split his chin wide open. We rushed him to the emergency room for treatment, and when the doctor there heard him crying, he said, "What do we have here, a little girl? Boys don't cry in my emergency room."

When we were first married, my husband's typical response whenever I became upset over a situation would be, "Why do you always have to make a mountain out of molehill? Why does everything have to be such a big deal?"

About that time, I saw a film called *The Pawnbroker* starring Rod Steiger. It was about a man who had lost his entire family in a concentration camp. As a result of that experience, the man became numb and unfeeling. He came to America, where he became a pawnbroker, an occupation that seemed to require someone with no feelings. Over time, he developed a relationship with a young boy, and when the boy died at the end of the film, the pawnbroker, unable to feel pain at the boy's death, pressed his hand down on a letter spindle until it went through his hand, just so that he could feel something. After seeing that movie, whenever my husband responded to me coldly, I would reply, "I forgot, you're the pawnbroker. You don't know how to feel."

Now, of course, I understand that my husband started out in life feeling just as deeply as anyone else, but he was forced to deny his feelings because it wasn't acceptable for a man to show his feelings.

Many men have told me that they have trouble showing their feelings because of their early childhood experiences. For example, Leon told me his father called him a sissy and a crybaby every time he cried. He wanted his father's acceptance, so he soon learned not to cry.

Kirk said that as a young boy, he ran to his mother for comfort every time he was frightened. His older brother, whom he idolized, teased him and called him a "mama's boy" or a "scaredy cat," so Kirk quickly learned to stop going to his mother for solace and to rely on himself.

Charlie remembers the first time his Dad took him hunting. "I hated the idea of killing or hurting anything, but Dad kept calling me a chicken," Charlie told the class.

"I wanted my father's approval so much that I pushed down my feelings and shot that rifle." Charlie ended by saying, "Today, I actually do enjoy hunting."

As children, you are told by the people you want to please the most that when someone calls you a name it's not supposed to matter, that "Sticks and stones may break your bones, but names will never harm you." Wrong! Names do hurt.

In addition, when your hurt feelings are not validated, you push them down in an attempt to be loved and accepted, and instead end up feeling isolated, angry, and guilty.

THE GREAT COVER-UP

Even many women have difficulty showing their feelings. Depending on how authoritarian your household was as you were growing up, you are either a person who can easily tap into your feelings or you're not.

It's so common for children to be taught to cover up their feelings that most of the time it goes unnoticed. For example, a child has just had an argument with her sister and her mother insists that she "march right over there and tell your sister you're sorry."

The child probably has a lot of feelings, but sorry isn't one of them.

She has to make a decision. Does she say, "No, I'm not sorry and I'm not going to say that I am," or does she march over there and say she's sorry so that she will have Mother's love and approval? My guess is that most children do the latter.

If, as a child, you cried when you were taken to a doctor's office for a shot, you were probably told, "There's nothing to be afraid of. This isn't going to hurt." When it did hurt, you cried even harder, while your mother and the doctor told you you were being silly.

Do you see how we start to cover up our feelings?

DEALING WITH GUILT

Parents have lots of ways to make their children feel guilty. Often, guilt is nothing more than not feeling the way that someone else says you should feel. If, for example, as a child you were told that it was wrong to hate someone, and you really hated little Marie next door, you would have felt guilty for having a feeling that your parents said you shouldn't have.

My parents came from Europe and had very little money. Every penny they earned went toward the expense of raising and educating my brother and me. They never spent anything on themselves, and I was constantly reminded how hard it was to earn money and how easy it was to spend. As a result, I feel guilty every time I buy anything for myself. The interesting thing is that I can spend money on my children or my husband with no guilt at all. I only feel guilty when it comes to spending on myself. So every time I'm waiting in line to pay for a new dress or a pair of shoes, I feel guilty. Every time my husband and I go on vacation without the children I feel guilty, because my parents never took a vacation. They always said, "Someday when the children are grown, we'll go on a vacation, but right now there's too much that needs to be done for us to be able to enjoy ourselves." (They were definitely people who postponed happiness.)

I've learned how to deal with my guilt, and I hope I can help you deal with yours. Whenever something makes me feel guilty, I just feel the guilt and do it anyway! Now you could spend the next five years going to therapy three times a week to erase the tapes from your mother, your father, your minister, priest, or rabbi, or anyone else who had a part in making you feel guilty. But, believe me, it would cost far less to go ahead and do whatever it is you're feeling guilty about than it would to go to therapy. So don't get rid of guilt! Keep it. Just feel the guilt and do it anyway.

A VERY EXPENSIVE GUILT TRIP

Another way to look at guilt is to compare the behaviors that result from guilt versus those that result from anger. Here's how it works: Every time we deny our own feelings, we feel angry. For example, if you really want to take a vacation but don't because you'd feel too guilty for spending the time and the money, you'll feel angry instead. If you don't buy that gorgeous dress because it's too expensive, you'll feel angry. Let's take a look at how we behave when we feel guilty versus how we behave when we feel angry.

I have back problems, and being in a Jacuzzi always makes me feel better. I wanted very much to have a spa put in our backyard, but my husband hates hot water and felt it would be a waste of money. Besides, he said, "We pay dues for the use of our association's clubhouse, which already has a spa."

Well, I don't feel like going to the clubhouse and meeting the entire neighborhood when my back is out. So finally I said, "I really want to get a spa. It would help a great deal with my back pain, and I feel I deserve it."

My husband's ungracious response was, "Fine, go ahead and get one! Just don't use the word 'we' when you explain the reason for getting it. If you want it, then it's your responsibility, not mine."

Until just a few years before, I wouldn't have dreamed of getting anything unless he wanted it as much as I did. But if you understand the concept that opposites attract, you'll realize that the chances of him wanting something as much as I do are about a thousand to one. We are different people. He doesn't experience back pain; I do. So, not only did I get a spa, I decided to landscape the entire backyard as well—including decking. We are talking about thousands of dollars worth of guilt—not a hundred dollars for a new outfit or fifty dollars for a perm—but thousands of dollars! Let's see what I did because of guilt:

- I thanked my husband at least three times a day for the wonderful gift I gave myself. I'd say, "You are the most wonderful husband in the world. I know you didn't want the spa, but you allowed me the space to do what I wanted."
- I sent little thank-you cards to his office and left little notes around the house.
- For at least three months, I was the greatest sex partner ever. Guilt has a way of turning you on. I always tell my students in the men's classes if they want a woman to respond to them sexually, make her feel guilty. Buy her gifts, take her on vacation, and shower her with surprises.
- I prepared the most beautiful romantic dinners imaginable.

My behavior reinforced him for allowing me to make my own decision based on my needs and wants. Remember, behavior that is reinforced is more likely to be repeated.

Now let's examine what behavior I would have exhibited had I not gotten the spa and felt angry:

- Since I'd be feeling that I didn't count and that all my husband cared about was himself, I certainly wouldn't thank him for anything.
- There'd be no notes, because I'd be angry and certainly couldn't express love.
- I'd probably have a headache and any other symptom I could think of to prevent lovemaking. Women who are angry can't respond sexually. If he touched me, I'd have what I call the "creepy crawlers."

Did my husband benefit from the spa? You bet he did, and if you asked him which feels better, to have a wife who is angry or a wife who is guilty, he wouldn't hesitate—the verdict would be guilty!

THEY CAN GET BY WITHOUT YOU

Earlier I said there are lots of ways that our parents can make us feel guilty. Well, being a parent can make us feel guilty too. In fact, sometimes I think that when a woman gives birth, she not only gets rid of the afterbirth, she rids herself forever of the feelings I want, I need, I deserve.

When my children were ten, nine, and seven years old, my husband and I decided to take a cruise. We were to be gone a total of eight days—longer than we had ever been gone before. We had taken a weekend away or an overnight getaway, but never eight days. My son was very upset that we were going and cried the night before and the morning we left. Once again I was feeling guilty. But I felt the guilt and did it anyway.

I felt I was such a good mother the other fifty-one weeks of the year that I didn't think it was really going to kill the children if I left them for a week. Those were my true feelings—not those of my parents, my friends, or my neighbors, but mine!

We went, and because of guilt, I bought each of the children presents in every port. When we returned from our cruise, my love cup was full, and I took them shopping for school clothes, let them have their friends sleep over, and spent lots of quality time with each of them. Had I not gone, my cup would have been empty and I would have been angry. I would have resented them and complained about how inconsiderate they were. No way would I have let them have sleep-over parties and stay up all hours of the night. Now, if my children were asked to choose between a mother who was angry and a mother who was guilty, which do you think they'd choose? Guilty, of course. Look how much they benefited from my guilt.

One day, while I was shopping at the mall, I felt a tap on my shoulder. I turned and saw a former student, looking absolutely wonderful. When I told her how great she looked, she whispered that she had taken my advice.

"I had wanted to get an eyelift for a very long time," she confided to me.

"But I always felt guilty about how much it would cost. Last month I decided to feel the guilt and do it anyway, and I'm really glad I did."

"My husband thinks I look wonderful too," she added.

Another student wrote to tell me that she had always wanted to have her breasts enlarged. She said that about a month after taking Light His Fire, she and her husband decided together what size she should be.

"I've never been happier about my body," she wrote. "Although I felt guilty about spending the money, I have no regrets. My husband loves the new me, and he's reaping the benefits of my guilt on a regular basis."

If you are angry because you are denying your feelings, I want you to trade your anger for guilt. And then, I want you to feel the guilt and do it anyway.

COVERED-UP FEELINGS CAUSE DISEASE

Covering up feelings is another form of lying. And like lying, we do it to protect someone we love or to protect ourselves. Warning: Covering up feelings—or not being true to your feelings—can be harmful to your health. If we examine the word *disease* carefully, we see that it is composed of *dis* and *ease*. And when we are not at ease, we get disease. We are all exposed to the same viruses and germs, but the people who get sick are usually those who are under a great deal of stress. My gynecologist tells me that he can safely predict that after the holidays the office will be filled with women with some kind of vaginal infection. Sure, they got through the holidays, but the stress caused them to become ill.

For most of us, there are just too many "shoulds" and "have tos," and not enough real choices. And adults aren't the only ones who experience stress— children are stressed too. That's why I have always allowed my children to take a "well day" off once in a while instead of waiting until they are sick to stay home. Sometimes just taking the day off and going to lunch with me is enough to make them feel good again. When a mother says her child was healthy the entire summer and now that school's started he's sick, she needs to examine what stress the child may be under.

The next time you or someone you love gets sick,

ask *what purpose this illness serves*. Some possible answers might be:

- I really didn't want to go to that function.
- I really didn't want the family over for the holidays.
- I really hate my job.
- I really want more love and attention.
- I really wanted to get out of the situation I'm in and I didn't know of any other way.
- I want sympathy.

Instead of waiting to take a day off from work until you have a fever and are too sick to move, why not take a day off when you're feeling great? Go shopping, go for a long walk on the beach, or just sit home and "vegetate." That old adage "An ounce of prevention is worth a pound of cure" really fits here. I really believe if you take a day off when you begin to feel stressed, you'll have fewer sick days, and so will your children.

THE BIG "C"

Cancer is a dreaded disease that has touched the lives of nearly everyone in some way. Most of us know someone who either suffers from or has died of cancer. And it seems that the reaction to hearing someone has cancer is always similar: "Oh, no, not 'so and so.' He's one of the kindest, most loving human beings alive. He'd give anyone the shirt off his back." Typically, cancer patients have denied their own feelings for the sake of others, a tendency that serves to make them well liked.

In his book *Natural Healing*, Mark Bricklen states that scientists have discovered that one of the characteristics of the cancer patient is "a tendency to harbor resentment and an impairment in his ability to express hostility." No wonder cancer patients are so likable. They never make waves!

In *Love, Medicine & Miracles*, Dr. Bernie Siegel cites the work of Dr. Caroline Bendel Thomas of Johns Hopkins University Medical School, who did a personality profile of 1,337 medical students and surveyed their health every decade throughout their adult lives. She was surprised to find that almost all of those who developed cancer "had throughout their lives been restricted in expressing emotion, especially aggressive emotions related to their own needs." According to Siegel, in order for cancer patients to get well, they need to see "how the needs of others, seen as the only ones that count, are used to cover up one's own." He goes on to say that for healing to occur, our outer choices have to match our inner desires, so that the energy that was used for these contradictions can now be used for healing.

Cancer patients are givers—not takers—a trait that is especially encouraged in women. A hospital nurse I know who works exclusively with cancer patients told me that they are the most pleasant and easygoing patients to care for, because they always put the needs of others before their own. While other patients start ringing for the nurse if their dinner tray is five minutes late, cancer patients don't even complain when their food is an hour late! They also play down their pain or their fear because they don't want to worry or upset anyone else.

I remember reading about another study of two hundred women who needed breast biopsies. Interestingly, the majority of women who complained, whined, and cried to anyone who would listen about the surgery they needed were cancer-free, while the majority of those who told no one other than their immediate families because they didn't want a fuss made over them were found to have cancer. I'd rather see just ten people at your funeral who loved you unconditionally than two hundred people who loved you because you always gave. In the first case, you'd probably outlive anybody who might come to your funeral, and in the second you might not live to be fifty!

One thing is for sure: If you are expressing your feelings, you will not be loved, or even liked, by everyone. A relationship lost because of honesty wasn't worth having to begin with. The cost of trying to please everyone is too great—*the cost could be your life!*

JUST SAY NO

It's human nature to take advantage of people who will allow you to. For instance, if I am stuck at a meeting or delayed in traffic and couldn't get to school in time to pick up my son, I might call a neighbor and ask a favor of her. If one neighbor says, "Sure, I'll pick him up, but next time try and give me a little more notice; we're right in the middle of dinner, and the other neighbor simply says, "Sure, where is he?" which one do you think I'll call on the next time I need a favor? The one who made it easy for me, of course. That's perfectly normal. What's abnormal is to allow yourself to be taken advantage of. If you don't look out for yourself, no one else will. You have to be the one to say no.

About a year after she graduated from Light His Fire, Darlene returned to tell me how much she had changed. Prior to taking the class, Darlene was a self-described "superwoman." She worked full time, she was president of a women's group, she volunteered her time for school fund-raisers, she was a devoted mother to two teenagers, and she and her husband seemed to have a perfect marriage.

What she learned in my class was that by giving so much to everyone else, she had become a very busy, well-organized, sacrificing woman who had forgotten how to have fun or enjoy life. She needed to be able to say no.

As Darlene reflected on her situation, she slowly began to make some changes. Now, a year later, she still has her job, which she loves, but she has curtailed most of her other activities.

"I have given myself permission to say no," she told me, "and in doing so, I am much more relaxed and playful."

Darlene's husband found it hard to adjust to her new playfulness at first, but he has grown to like this new aspect of her personality and has learned to enjoy their time together more.

Sometimes we have trouble saying no because we aren't clear in our own minds about what we're willing to do. I've found that one of the simplest ways to determine how much you want to do something is to use a scale of one to ten. Let's say you've been asked to join a bowling team. That's easy—if, on a scale of one to ten it's a two, don't join—I don't care if all your neighbors are joining.

This method has been very useful in helping my husband and me understand just how the other feels about a shared activity. For example, if we have been invited to a dinner party, we'll say, "On a scale of one to ten, how much do you want to go?" If I say three and he says one, we don't go. If, on the other hand, he says nine and I say three, I'd probably go to please him. If a movie I want to see is a ten, he'd go with me even though the same movie might only be a four for him. Before we started using this method, we frequently assumed we were pleasing the other by going to a particular function, when, in fact, that function was very low on the scale for both of us.

Once you determine that you don't want to do something, the key is to just say no—and then be quiet. Don't say no and then give a hundred excuses. If someone calls and asks for a donation, for example, and you want to give, then give. If you really don't want to, then just say, "No. I'm sorry, I'm not interested," and then be quiet. The person on the other end isn't going to say, "How dare you!" What you'll hear is, "Oh, okay. Thank you." And don't bake five thousand cookies for the bake sale just because no one else will. That's not a good enough reason. You decide what you want. Your life depends on it!

ASK AND YOU SHALL RECEIVE

A common attitude among women is that their men should somehow magically know what it is they want or need. They believe if they have to tell a man what makes them happy, it diminishes them in some way. Women who attend my class learn to replace that mistaken belief with a more accurate viewpoint. The only way to get what you want is to ask for it! Men are not mind readers, and they don't have ESP. They have to be told what you need to make you happy. As I tell my students, ask and you shall receive!

Don't be like Joan, who was exhausted on one particular Friday and really wanted some time alone with her husband, Bill. When Bill called that afternoon, instead of suggesting they get a baby-sitter for the evening and go to dinner alone, she asked, "Would you like to go out with just me or should we make it a family dinner?"

Unfortunately, Bill made the wrong choice and replied, "Let's bring the kids. That would be nice."

Joan was angry all day, and by the time they got to the restaurant that evening, her husband had asked her what was wrong at least half a dozen times. Her reply was always "Nothing." She remained silent all through dinner as the kids and their dad talked.

Later that evening, as Joan was getting ready for bed, she shouted at her husband, "You can't really love me if you never want to be alone with me!"

Shocked, Bill asked, "What are you talking about?"

Joan finally explained that she had needed time alone with him and that she hadn't wanted the children to accompany them that evening.

Bill responded by saying that he too would have preferred to be alone with her, but he was afraid she would think he was selfish, so he included the children. Bill wasn't a mind reader. Joan needed to tell him exactly what she wanted. This would have been a great time to use the scale of one to ten.

MIXED MESSAGES

Another mistake women tend to make is to send mixed messages. They say one thing and mean another. For example, when my husband and I were first married and were somewhat strapped for money, I used to say, "Let's not get each other anything for this anniversary," and he believed I meant what I said. Then the day of our anniversary would arrive and I would present him with a gift, but he would have nothing for me! Why not? Because I had asked for nothing. For the next few days, I'd cry and be miserable and ask, "How could you have believed me?"

And he'd respond, "But you said we shouldn't get each other anything!"

I should have said what I really meant: "Since we don't have a lot of money, let's just get each other a small token of our love. It doesn't have to be expensive. It really means a lot to me to get a card and something I know is from your heart."

Lots of women send mixed messages. Sondra told the class about the time she had to have some wisdom teeth pulled. Her husband offered to take the day off from work so he could be there for her and take her home, but Sondra insisted that it was "no big deal" and that her girlfriend could take her home much more easily.

"Well," Sondra told the class, "it was a big deal. When I woke up, I felt awful, I was lonely, and I wanted my husband there to hold my hand."

Later that night, Sondra attacked her husband, saying angrily, "I needed you. Why weren't you there for me? You should have known I didn't really want to be there alone."

Needless to say, Sondra's husband was a very confused man at this point.

My favorite story comes from Patty, who learned not to send mixed messages the hard way. A few years ago, Patty's in-laws were scheduled to visit for a week. As luck would have it, her husband, Chris, had scheduled a weekend fishing trip just prior to the Monday his parents were to arrive.

Chris volunteered to cancel his trip, but Patty gamely told him she wouldn't think of it, assuring him that she could handle the housework and shopping on her own. As the weekend wore on, however, Patty wore out. By Sunday afternoon she was tired, angry, and lonely. She hated her in-laws, she hated her husband, and she hated her house.

Late Sunday afternoon Patty slipped on the garage stairs as she carried out the last load of trash, and she was tired and hurting when Chris arrived home, late Sunday night, to find Patty, her leg in a cast, crying her eyes out.

"I don't understand it, Patty," he said, shaking his head. "Why did you tell me to go if you knew you were going to have so much to do and you really needed me to help?''

Like many women, Patty thought her husband should have known what she wanted. ''It seemed pretty obvious to me that he should have stayed home to help. It was his parents who were coming, and he knew there was a lot to do!''

Well, ladies, take it from me—and from Patty, and all the other women who have learned the hard way. Men can't read your minds. They don't have ESP! A man won't have the foggiest idea what you want, unless you tell him.

I never send messages anymore that I don't really mean. The cost of doing so is too great.

WHAT DO YOU WANT FROM ME?

Most men feel completely helpless when a woman shows extreme emotion. They just don't know how to deal with it. But when your mate asks you in frustration, ''What do you want from me?'' you need to postpone your answer to a time when he is really going to listen. Timing is very important when you are talking about your wants, needs, or feelings.

John, a student in my men's class, volunteered that he felt fortunate to know what his wife wanted when she was upset, because when they first got married, she told him that if she was ever depressed or angry to put her in the car and take her to the beach. Because she had taken the time to explain what she needed when they were both calm and receptive, whenever a crisis occurred or something happened that they really needed to talk over, John knew to take her to the beach, which seemed to soothe her nerves and always calmed her down.

As simple as this may sound, most couples have no idea what to do for each other in times of stress or crisis, or in the face of a tragic event. Knowing that everyone is different, you need to tell your mate in a loving way what's best for you and to discuss what is best for him.

Some women want to be left alone when they are upset, some want their husbands to hold them, and others want to be asked, "What can I do to help?" For me personally, the most wonderful words I can hear when I'm in a "no cope" situation are, "Is there anything I can do to help?" and my husband knows it. I don't know why, but it always calms me down when I can think rationally of some tangible thing he can do to help me.

If you tell your man what you need at a time when you aren't upset, he'll store the information away, and when the time comes he'll remember it. So the next time you are together, say, "Honey, whenever I start to cry, it would mean so much if you were to put your arms around me and just hold me." Or, "The next time I get mad, just give me fifteen minutes to blow off steam and then we can talk about it when I calm down." I believe each of us knows what it is that we need. We just need to take the time to think about it and learn to express it.

WISH LIST

A wonderful way to bring greater intimacy to your relationship and to get your needs met is for each of you to make a wish list and then share it with each other. On it put down anything your husband can give you that would bring you more joy and let him do the same. For example, many years ago I told my husband I wanted a surprise. Because he is very logical, he wanted to know what kind of surprise I had in mind. I replied, "It wouldn't be much of a surprise if I told you. I don't care. Anything that you plan without me and that I don't know about would qualify."

I told him he had thirty years to work on it, but he had to promise that before I died he'd plan a surprise. One night about six months later, I came home and found his mother sitting in our living room. Totally surprised, I exclaimed, "Gee, how did you get here?"

My husband jumped out of his hiding place and yelled, "It's your surprise!" He had called his mother to baby-sit, bought me the most beautiful nightgown I had ever seen (it's still my favorite), packed it in an overnight case, made dinner reservations at a beautiful restaurant, and made arrangements for us to spend the night at a hotel.

He had never done anything like this for me before, and I had a wonderful time letting him take care of everything. Usually it was up to me to find the baby-sitter and make the reservations. This was certainly a welcome change.

I also asked him to meet me for lunch once in a while. It was exciting to meet midday and flirt over lunch with my husband, and it made me feel important to know that I was on his calendar. We started our rendezvous years ago, and to this day we still go out for lunch together at least once a month.

In addition, I requested that he send me flowers once in a while. "But they're so expensive," he said, "and then they just die."

I told him that flowers represented romance and were not something I would buy for myself. To me, flowers meant "I'm thinking of you." I told him I didn't want them all of the time, just when we'd had a beautiful evening the night before or when he was especially looking forward to being with me. A couple of weeks after my request he brought home a beautiful bouquet of flowers—the first of many.

I used to envy my neighbor, because whenever she had us over for dinner, I noticed that her husband would be the first to thank her for all her time and trouble, ranting and raving about how delicious the food was. The best I could get from my husband when I cooked a big dinner was, "It's okay, food is food. If you want to make it again, go ahead." How depressing! I decided to ask for a thank you on my wish list.

I told my husband I didn't expect thanks when I threw something together, but when I spent hours in the kitchen preparing a meal I really needed to hear that he and the children appreciated it. We always teach our children to thank others for a meal—why shouldn't mothers get the same courtesy?

The next evening at dinner, I heard him whisper to the children, "Okay, when I count to three, say, 'Thank you, Mommy. That was delicious,' " And then in unison they all shouted, "Thank you, Mommy.

That was delicious!" I kissed each of the children and thanked them for the compliment. I also kissed my husband and thanked him for remembering my feelings. Remember, if you don't reinforce a new behavior, you'll never see the new behavior again. Even though at the time it was phony and contrived, it quickly became completely automatic for my children to thank me whenever I would prepare a nice dinner.

I hope you are beginning to see that my husband brings home flowers, takes me on surprise getaways, and meets me for lunch, because I asked for it. I didn't just happen to get a wonderful man who catered to my every need. I have requested everything! There's no need to envy me. What worked for me will work for you too.

Put whatever it is you want in writing, whether it's a picnic once a month, going to the movies every Sunday night, or a big kiss hello every night. No matter what your wishes are, you must be able to let your mate know. So, get out your pen and paper and start writing your wish list.

MAKE A WISH

The following are some of the wishes women in my classes have put on their lists:

- Take a walk with me after dinner three times a week.
- Give me a real kiss hello and good-bye, instead of a peck on the cheek.

- Take me out for a date once a week. You make the plans.
- Send me a "no occasion" gift just to say you love me. It doesn't have to be expensive.
- Ask me out to lunch.
- Tell me you love me at least three times a day.
- Send me flowers and a sexy note at the office once in a while. I want everyone to envy me.
- Call just to tell me you love me.
- Help me with the chores. Let's make a list and divide it evenly.
- Hold me, touch me, and kiss me at times other than when we are making love.

Some of the things men have put on their wish lists are:

- Stop what you are doing to greet me when I come home in the evening, instead of telling me you'll be with me in a minute.
- Take the initiative in lovemaking. Tell me what you want.
- Allow me to watch sports on TV without a hassle.
- Give me time to unwind when I come home from work before expecting me to engage in conversation.
- Surprise me once in a while with a special dinner, soft music, and a sexy outfit.
- Allow me to have one day off a week with no chores or errands.
- Accompany me to a sports event once in a while. I'd really like you to join me.

- Write me secret notes that I'll find when I least expect them.

If both of you agreed to do your best to meet each other's wishes, your relationship couldn't help but be harmonious and romantic.

BABY TALK AND PET NAMES COME OUT OF THE CLOSET

Baby talk is not a subject that is usually addressed publicly, and I don't recall seeing it mentioned in any of the books I've read. It's not something women share with each other; in fact, most women don't analyze what they're doing at the time they're doing it.

Usually, when I ask a woman if she ever uses baby talk or pet names with her lover, she turns beet red, gets very flustered, and says she couldn't possibly talk about something so personal. Over the years, however, I have managed to gather enough information to share it with you here.

The stories that follow are very special to me, because I know how hard it was for these women to reveal this aspect of themselves. This is the kind of talk that goes on behind closed doors. Although women find it easy to talk with one another about many things, baby talk and pet names is not one of them, but I think it's time for all women to know why some men feel so deeply captivated and contented with the women in their lives.

Before I started teaching Light His Fire, I had always assumed that everyone talked baby talk at one time or another, but I learned that I was wrong. Many of the women in my classes have asked me to make a tape specifically on baby talk, because they never heard their mothers or fathers speak this way.

Talking baby talk and using pet names is a great tool when:

- Your mate is too serious.
- Your mate is ignoring you.
- You really want to do something your mate doesn't want to do.
- You want something very much.

It's very hard to put in writing what I usually demonstrate in the classroom verbally and visually, but I'll do my best. To practice this type of behavior, you have to think about how you'd talk to a puppy or tiny baby. You sweeten your voice, maybe raising the pitch a little, at the same time making exaggerated facial expressions.

Suppose your feelings are hurt or you're disappointed. Usually, if you pout, sticking out your lower lip, and say nothing, your mate will immediately ask, "What's the matter?"

In a tiny, barely audible voice, you might answer, "I want to hide in your suitcase and go with you on this trip."

Although you might not get to go, his reaction will be, "You sweet thing. I wish you could go too."

One of my students was a very strong, high-powered woman who had frequent arguments with her mate—an equally strong, opinionated man—that usually ended with them not speaking to each other for days. After the class on baby talk, she called to tell me how pouting had really worked for her. Pat's husband refused to go into a movie if it had already started. Once the credits started showing on the screen, he'd wait for the second show. He never deviated from this rule.

Pat had waited for weeks to see Alan Alda's movie *The Four Seasons.* When they finally got to the ticket counter, after waiting in line for some time, her husband made an about-face and started walking away.

When she asked why, he replied, "It's too late. It just started, and you know the rule."

She shouted, "Can't you break the rule just this once?" and he shouted back, "NO!"

Pat told me that ordinarily a scene such as this would have resulted in a two-day silence. Instead, when they got in the car, she turned to him and stuck out her lower lip in a pout.

He looked at her and said, "You're so adorable. You really want to see that picture? Okay, let's go in."

Pat said she almost burst out laughing. She couldn't believe what had happened, and once inside the movie theater, she excused herself and went to the ladies' room and laughed hysterically.

Jan, who was also a very independent woman, told us that she made a hobo knapsack for herself and her dog. It consisted of a long stick with a bundle tied to one end. Whenever her boyfriend got mad at her, she'd stick one knapsack in the dog's collar, and holding the other one over her shoulder, she'd walk past her boyfriend and say, in a baby voice, "Come on, Fifi, we're gonna run away from home and go where we're wuved. No one around here wuvs us." Her boyfriend would take one look at this pathetic sight and burst out laughing.

BABY GAMES

Some brave women have told me they play baby games with their mates. They say it's a great way to alleviate the tension and worry that many men bring home with them from work. Shelley told me that whenever her husband comes home irritable or tense, she says to him, in baby, talk, "Come to mama and let's rock-a-bye, baby."

Then, lying on the bed, she cradles her husband in her arms as she rocks and sings, "Rock-a-bye, baby, in the treetop," to him until he relaxes.

Eva plays "Wind, Wind Little Baby" with her husband to help him unwind. She actually holds his arms and rotates them in a winding motion as she sings, "Wind, wind little baby, wind, wind, little baby, pull, pull, and clap, clap, clap."

Eva says her husband always smiles and laughs at the end of the song.

PET NAMES

Pet names are another way of being playful. One of my students said that when her mother died, her dad wandered around in a daze, saying, "Now whose Pookey Bear will I be?" Her mother had always called him "Pookey Bear." She shouted, "My Pookey Bear is home!" whenever he came home, and he'd always say, "Stop it, Grace. You're embarrassing me." Secretly though, he loved it, and when she was gone, he mourned the loss of his pet name as well as the loss of his wife.

Allison told me her husband is the only man in the neighborhood who willingly takes the garbage out every week. The other women on the block, having watched this man whistle as he moves the garbage cans from the garage to the sidewalk for years, have even asked Allison what her secret is.

"I would never tell them, of course," Allison said, as she told her secret to the class. "It would really embarrass my husband.

"I never wanted to have to take the trash out myself, so early in our marriage I started a ritual that continues to this day," said Allison.

Every Wednesday night, when it's time to take out the trash, Allison turns to her husband, Mac, and in a deep, loud voice says, "Who's going to save the day and take out the garbage for Minnie Mouse? Why, it's Mighty Mouse—to the rescue."

Mac always grins as Allison feels his biceps and says in a squeaky little voice, "Ooh, Mighty Mouse is sooo strong!"

Amy also used a fictional character in a cute way to get her husband to do things around the house. If she needed the trim on the house painted, for example, she would say, "Faster than a speeding bullet—who's going to paint my trim? It's Superman!"

Clara referred to her husband as Captain Marvel. These clever women have learned how to make a

man want to please them by emphasizing their masculinity in a playful way.

PICK A PET NAME

The following is a list of pet names that I have heard
from women over the years. Of course, there were
many more, but I have chosen those that could easily
be used or understood by most people. Many were
omitted because they were only meaningful to the
two people involved.

Teddy Bear Tiger	Baby Duck	Stud Dumpling
Lover Buns	Hon Bun	Love Bucket
Pussy Cat	Poopsie	Stud Muffin
Snookums	Sweet Cake	Sunshine
Lovey Dovey	Sweet Pea	Lambie Pie
Pumpkin	Sweet Cheeks	Lover Boy
Nummy Num	Tiger Lover	Butter Butt
Sugar Pot	Knucklenuts	Pudding Pie
Hunkey Poo	Hunky Punky	Honey Buns
Tootsie Wootsie	Dr. Nude	Apple Dumpling
Bubba Bear	Big Kahuna	Peaches

The world might be shocked to discover that many
prominent men who are referred to by the highly re-
spected title of Doctor, Senator, or even President,
may very well be called sweet cheeks, lover buns, or
stud muffin by their sweethearts!

PLAYFULNESS SAVES THE DAY

Many women have meekly shared that when they've bought something that cost too much, childish behavior has saved the day, and my childish behavior has broken the tension in my own home on more than one occasion. For example, there was the time that I wanted to see *Man of La Mancha* and tickets were hard to get. So I bought the tickets at an agency and paid fifty dollars each for them. I knew my husband would be upset at how much I had spent on the tickets. He was away on a business trip, and when he called that night, I resorted to baby talk. In a little girl voice, I said, "I've been a bad, bad girl. I bought tickets to see *Man of La Mancha* and you're going to be very mad at me when I tell you how much they cost, but I promise I'll kiss you from the tippie of your head to the tippie of your toes if you don't get mad."

He started laughing, and said, "From the tippie of my head to the tippie of my toes, huh? Well, maybe it will be worth it."

See what I mean? Baby talk saved the day.

Other women have resorted to blaming a make-believe character when something they do upsets their husband, using phrases like "Alf would let me," or "Alf made me do it."

Another student told the class how jealous she was of their dog. Every night when her husband came home, the dog would lie down and turn over on its back. Ignoring his wife, her husband would get down on the floor and pet and play with the dog. One night she decided to be playful, and when her husband came in the door, she was down on her back waving her arms and kicking her legs, imitating the dog. Her husband responded by getting down and kissing and playing with her. In a nonverbal way, my student had shown her husband that she wanted the same greeting he gave the dog.

BEHIND EVERY MAN HIDES A LITTLE BOY

Most men can't resist that vulnerable little girl who resides inside all of us, but I have found that most women who were only children or the oldest in the family have a tough time being playful or using baby talk. If you heard messages such as, "Grow up and act your age," or "Stop being a baby," it may be hard for that little girl to come out. You have to experiment with what feels comfortable for you.

Practice looking adorable in front of a mirror. I know that what I've said here feels foreign to some of you, but I'm convinced that men will react favorably to you if you can make them laugh or appeal to the little boy in them. Remember, inside every man, no matter how strong, how successful, or how powerful he is, is a little boy just waiting for permission to come out and play.

In fact, one of my students said her boyfriend asked her to marry him because she was the only woman who could play with him. He told her, "Your little girl makes my little boy want to play, and it feels so satisfying."

Some men in my classes have felt comfortable revealing how much they love the playfulness in their mate.

Wade, for example, is a doctor who said, "All day long I am a competent, efficient, and responsible adult. I love to come home, close the door behind me, and be able to loosen up.

"My wife, Marilyn, is the only woman I've ever known who could make me laugh with her silly make-believe characters and little-girl games. I love every minute of it."

I know a lot of you feel that this kind of playfulness is too out of character for you to try, but it's very important to learn how to let the child inside you come out. Even though it's hard, try at least one new behavior and watch the results.

ACTION ASSIGNMENT #6

- **Share your feelings without attacking.**
  Your feelings are never wrong. Stand behind them.

- **Make it safe for you to be told the truth.**
  Tell your mate from now on you'll never be angry at him for telling you the truth.

- **Trade anger for guilt.**

- **Just say no.**
  Practice saying no to activities that don't interest you.

- **Ask for what you want.**
  Make it easy for your husband to meet your needs. Tell him what you want.

- **Don't send mixed messages.**
  Be honest about what you want. Tell the truth.

- **Make a wish list.**
  Have your mate make one too. Read the lists to each other and discuss them.

- **Be playful.**
  Use pet names, baby talk, and games to release the children inside you both.

MARRIAGE VOWS FOR A LASTING LOVE

(To be read by both the Bride and the Groom)

I PROMISE—to love you always for who you are and never to ask you to be who you are not.

I PROMISE—to respect the fact that your ideas and opinions may be different from mine, but hold as much truth and value for you as mine do for me.

I PROMISE—to verbalize and demonstrate my admiration, respect, and appreciation for you as a person.

I PROMISE—to care more about your feelings than about being right. To always listen without judging.

I PROMISE—to take responsibility for my own happiness and not expect you to provide it for me.

I PROMISE—to love myself, for the more I love myself, the more love I am able to give you.

I PROMISE—to acknowledge and honor my own feelings and to share them with you.

I PROMISE—to pay equal attention to both your emotional and physical need for closeness.

I PROMISE—to always treat you as the most important person in my life, because you are.

Conclusion
WHAT A DIFFERENCE A DAY MAKES

*C*ongratulations! You are a very special kind of woman. You are a woman who is always looking for ways to improve your life, yourself, and your relationship. Your man is very lucky to have you as the woman in his life. While other women whine and complain, you've done something positive to make your love affair last—you're ready to Light His Fire!

By now you should have a set of six large index cards, with reminders written on them to help keep you on track. If you haven't done it yet, buy the largest cards you can get and use the extras to copy what you've written for your friends, daughter, coworker, or any family member who doesn't know why her relationship isn't working. It just might be the most valuable gift they ever receive.

Now that you are organized with the knowledge

you need to change your life, it's time for *action*. Join me and the thousands of women who are now leading exciting lives in the romantic relationship of their dreams. Become part of that elite group of women who know how to keep a man hopelessly and passionately in love with them forever.

It will take work and effort on your part, but everything worthwhile does. You will reap the rewards in direct relationship to your effort, and the fulfilling relationship you will achieve can never be taken away from you.

As you apply the principles in this book, you will see immediate results. The changes you seek will not take years, or even months to achieve. One day is all it will take to turn your life around!

The changes you seek will occur as soon as you implement the actions I have outlined. All you have to do is believe in yourself and the power you have as a woman.

Remember, love is never enough. You must verbalize and demonstrate your love for the man in your life over and over on a daily basis. Provide him with a safe, loving, and stimulating environment, and you will be a vital part of his happiness forever. A man who experiences this kind of love will never let you go.

Your Prince Charming is either right by your side, or standing close by just waiting to be discovered by you. Never give up believing in fairy tales. It is possible to live happily ever after! It will happen to you!

May all of your dreams come true—

Love,
Ellen

ABOUT THE AUTHOR

ELLEN KREIDMAN is the founder of the courses Light His Fire and Light Her Fire. For the past eight years she has been a dynamic public speaker who has motivated and educated thousands of men and women. She has a combined B.A. in psychology and education. She has had a twenty-three-year love affair with her husband and has three children. Ms. Kreidman lives in El Toro, California.